The Best Of COLORADO

Cover Art by Marcia Perry
Illustrated by Kevin Miller
Book and Cover Design by Bob Schram

PRUETT **P** PUBLISHING COMPANY
Boulder, Colorado

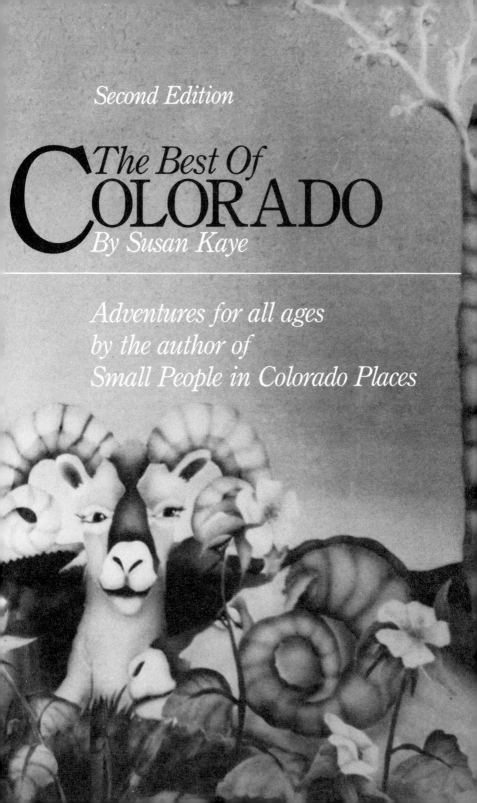

Second Edition

The Best Of
COLORADO

By Susan Kaye

*Adventures for all ages
by the author of
Small People in Colorado Places*

Second Edition
1 2 3 4 5 6 7 8 9

Printed in the United States of America

Library of Congress Cataloging-in-Publication Data

Kaye, Susan, 1945–
    The best of Colorado / by Susan Kaye.–2nd ed.
        p.   cm.
    "Adventures for all ages."

    Includes index.
    ISBN 0-87108-770-7 (pbk.)
    1. Colorado–Description and travel–1981–   –
Guide-books. I. Title.
F774.3.K39   1988
917.88′0433–dc19   88-18714
                                                   CIP

In memory of my father,
Ben Keppler

FOREWORD

How many times have you traveled Colorado highways, heading for a few days' getaway, only to arrive and wonder "Now what?"

You choose some promising restaurants, stroll the town, buy ice cream cones and souvenirs, perhaps ride a horse, and call it a vacation. Precious holiday moments become not unlike John Denver's sensitive lyrics about working all day, going home, and having nothing to say.

Yet the possibilities for Colorado adventures are overwhelming.

• Photograph an eerie ghost town that teeters on the Continental Divide.

• Ride a donkey-pulled cart deep into a mountain crisscrossed with veins of gold and silver.

• Ascend a hand-crafted thirty-two-foot ladder to an Anasazi cave home.

• Climb aboard a 100-year-old narrow gauge train that steams deep into the San Juan wilderness.

With a surfeit of available experiences, it's easy to miss the very best. That's why I've written *The Best of Colorado.*

The problem is not finding something to do, but finding the activities and sites you'll most enjoy. Planning a holiday by reading the glowing adjectives of brochures can be risky. The tedious, brief "listings" format used by most guidebooks is equally chancy.

The Best of Colorado presents detailed information about towns, mines, museums, historic spots, and resorts in a casual, lighthearted style. My goal has been to share my first-hand impressions, trivial and otherwise, with readers so they'll be well acquainted with a destination even before they arrive. This is the same narrative approach that readers responded to so favorably in my earlier Front Range family guide, *Small People in Colorado Places.*

More than just a list of popular areas, this imaginative guide helps you enjoy Colorado's best even more. Learn about the Swedish cook at Keystone who sat on his roof to survey his cabbage patch, or the four-foot-long marble soda fountain in Merriam's Drug Store, South Park City. These are the details often missed by guidebooks and tourists alike, the details that help make fond memories.

This unique guide identifies the places that will make each vacation day a special one. My native state became my textbook as I re-visited places I've known for a lifetime. Once again I toured the mines, hiked the trails, studied the exhibits, and talked to the people so I could share with you the hundreds of adventures that make Colorado such a special playground.

Imagination, careful observation, and an adventurous attitude are the keys to enjoying new places – whether you're walking the perimeter of a shy alpine lake or ballooning above the Elk Mountains of Pitkin County. Just finding and identifying wildflowers – with evocative names such as Shooting Star – could take up an entire summer. Then there are the ghost towns to explore, the mines to discover, the mountains to climb, and the wild animals to photograph. This book will help stimulate your imagination, whether you're wondering about Leadville's doomed Ice Palace or a life in a prairie sod house.

The joy of seeing a new site should begin with the reading – I hope you'll find that's true of *The Best of Colorado.*

CONTENTS

SOUTHWEST

Cliff-hanging Trains, Mysterious Indian Ruins, and Jeeping the Jagged San Juans:

WEST CENTRAL

Gushing Hot Springs, Fire-red Layered Canyons, and Swanky Resorts:

NORTHWEST

Dinosaur Cemeteries, High Tundra Roads, and Cowboy Country:

CENTRAL ROCKIES

Hidden Mines, Mountains of Ski Slopes,
Gold Rush Bonanzas, and Haunting Ghost Towns:

DENVER–PLUS

Herds of Shaggy Buffalo, Dinosaur-filled Museums,
and Plowing Oxen Teams. What a City!

NORTHEAST

Land of Centennial*:*

SOUTHEAST

Buckskinned Trappers, America's Best-loved Mountain,
Trading Posts, Shifting Sand Dunes,
and the Thunder-Rumble of Narrow Gauges
through High Plateaus:

CHAPTER 1

SOUTHWEST

DURANGO
SILVERTON
OURAY
TELLURIDE
MONTROSE

Durango

Durango-Silverton Narrow Gauge_____

Summer, trains leave daily for the eight-hour round-trip ride to Silverton. Trains may also be boarded in Silverton. Durango ticket office: 247-2733. Summer reservations are highly advised.

☐ The plucky narrow gauge that steams back and forth to Silverton all summer keeps Durango on its toes. The first loud toot from the anxious engine behind the quaint, flower-trimmed wooden depot is before 7:30 A.M. No one within earshot of Main Avenue can use the old "sleeping in" excuse for being late – when the train rolls along the narrow tracks paralleling downtown, it proclaims its departure to the entire valley.

Just as in Silverton, the narrow gauge is the major focus of the tourist trade. The train's prominence in Durango's pattern of life is appropriate, since the town has always been first and foremost a railroad town. Durango was founded in 1880 by the Denver and Rio Grande, which incorporated its initials into the name.

Two years later, the rails were extended north through the tortuous Animas Canyon. The first passenger train arrived in Silverton in the summer of 1882; as might be expected, "a wild, hilarious time was enjoyed by the populace for several days" after the event.

The day-long round trip between Durango and Silverton is not exactly "wild and hilarious,"

but it is popular despite the coal fragments and
smoke belched onto heads, cameras, slacks,
and sandwiches throughout the trip. At the turn-
around point, a two-hour break allows time to
disembark, lunch, and browse.

Round-trip to Silverton is ninety miles. At an
average speed of sixteen miles an hour, it's a
long ride. It can be broken up by taking a bus
one way.

A taste of the West. Durango's Main Avenue has a definite western character, especially
on the west side of the street, with its two
grand Victorian hotels. The Strater Hotel boasts
the historic and opulent Diamond Belle Saloon
and the Diamond Circle Theater, which has had
melodrama for twenty-four years.

The dignified General Palmer House shares a
carefully landscaped block with the railway
depot. It is one of the few remaining railroad
hotels in the nation. A recent renovation puts
this grand, historic site back on the map.

A taste of chocolate. Thousands of
chocolate lovers are unwittingly indebted to
Durango for being the home of the Rocky
Mountain Chocolate Factory, with its caramel-
covered apples rolled in chocolate candies. One
of these treats is a not-to-be-forgotten vacation
indulgence.

Tracing history. Visit the site of the area's
first settlement, short-lived Animas City No. 1,
by following County Road 250 north from the
end of Thirty-second Street. At mile 11.7, the
road turns abruptly, leading to one-lane Baker's
Bridge, named after Charles Baker, an early
pioneer. The chasm was also the setting where
Robert Redford and Paul Newman made their
leap to the river in "Butch Cassidy and the Sun-
dance Kid."

Mesa Verde National Park _____

In the southwest corner of Colorado, 420 miles from Denver and 36 miles southwest of Durango. The park is open year-round. Accommodations, facilities, services, and commercial tours are available from early May to mid-October. Full interpretive services are offered only from mid-June through Labor Day.

☐ The park service outlines four different tours depending on available time: two hours, four hours, full day, and two days. Those who choose the four-hour option are compressing 330 years of history into each hour spent in Mesa Verde, and that's not allowing for time to park the car, feed the chipmunks, or gaze at the many-hued mesas.

The park and hundreds of square miles nearby were inhabited by prehistoric Pueblo Indians called Anasazi from about 2000 years ago until 1300 A.D. This is the only national park devoted to the work of people. Yet it's the closeness with nature, or perhaps a sense of the Anasazi's oneness with the arid environment, that is the overwhelming feature. This is a park to enjoy slowly, savoring the wonder of a civilization that survived here for so long, so primitively.

It's a pleasant surprise to find that the canyons have not been graded and asphalted into easily walked slopes. Instead, the park provides hand-fashioned ladders (including a thirty-two-foot-high ladder to Balcony House) and roughly done steps, such as those along the trail to Cliff Palace. This particular trail parallels one used by the Indians. Near the ladders are shallow hand and toe holds in the cliff wall, a common Anasazi method of ascending to the upper farmlands.

Cliff House is the largest site and the one so often pictured. Resist the temptation to head straight toward it, as it can be appreciated better if the developmental sequence of the area is first understood. That means visiting the well-done museum and following the Mesa Loop Road tour of the Mesa Top Ruins. Along the short road is evidence of six hundred years of cultural development before the cliff dwellings were built.

On the Loop Road is a view of the Navajo Canyon, which holds more than sixty cliff dwellings along its fifteen miles. Even though all of the park's six hundred sites have been long discovered, it's up to each visitor to rediscover them, excitedly pointing to the miniature dark windows that appear just under canyon rims.

Near the end of the drive is Sun Point Overlook, the best place for getting an overview of thirteenth-century Anasazi land. Seven major sites are visible, each painstakingly constructed of sandstone bricks the size of loaves of bread.

The Navajos call these long-gone people the "Anasazi," meaning Ancient Ones. We know hardly anything about them: where they came from, where they went, or why. We know they worked incredibly hard: farming, building, making baskets and pottery, and storing water for the hot summer. Before they learned to make pottery, they wove large baskets that served as their cupboards, wheelbarrows, jars, and even cooking utensils. Like the Navajos, they depended heavily on corn and no doubt relaxed with a hot cup of corn tea.

Religion must have ruled their lives, since kivas (underground ceremonial centers) are everywhere, even in relatively small sites. It's estimated that some 250 people lived in Cliff Palace. Since kivas were used only by the men, there was one kiva for every five men. These ceremonial centers had to be excavated, bricked, roofed, and furnished with benches; that's a lot of work just to get away from the women.

Brief but furious thunderstorms often interrupt afternoon sightseeing. Once they're over, the air is cooled, and the ruins glisten in the soft light. Two evening programs, timed so they can both be attended, continue the magical spell of this area. Morfield Campground has an evening campfire series, and Far View Lodge shows a multimedia production.

SILVERTON

The best way to see Bangkok is by boat, joining the throngs on the Chao Pryah River. The romantic introduction to San Francisco's hills is the trolley; London has its famous Cockney-guided boat trip down the Thames, past the Tower.

In Silverton, there is no best way. To arrive by either train or car is stupendous. The Million Dollar Highway, which connects Silverton with Durango and Ouray, is the most spectacular stretch of highway in Colorado. But the Silverton narrow gauge, running along the Los Animas River from Durango, passes through rugged wilderness famed throughout the nation.

In the city's early days, water barrels were delivered on a sled pulled by a dog team in winter and on a wagon in summer. By 1879 there was a population of 3000, and thirty-five saloons boasted they never closed their doors. But eventually Silverton began putting on "metropolitan airs"; in 1899 there was an objection to cows running loose on the streets.

Tourists are on the loose nowadays, as the Durango-Silverton Narrow Gauge trip from Durango includes a two-hour layover in Silverton. (During the summer, the train can be boarded in Silverton as well.) The layover includes just enough time for lunch, to hunt for an unusual specimen in one of the many rock shops, and to visit the San Juan Historical Society Museum in the jail building next to the Courthouse.

Jeeping. For those with more time, jeeping is a main attraction. San Juan County was once the home of many mining towns and camps. Some, like Eureka, can be reached by car; Mineral Point and Animas Forks require four-wheel drive. Jeep rental is available at a couple of locations. The Chamber of Commerce sells a jeep map in town or by mail for fifty cents. It includes a "circle jeep tour" brochure outlining the history of the different towns along the tour.

Hikes. Many day hikes originate from Silverton. A map at the information caboose on Blair Street marks close-in trails. The Christ of the Mines Shrine overlooks the town from Anvil Mountain; it is easily reached by foot.

OURAY

It's a little confusing to find Swiss window baskets and ornate, cutout railings in an out-of-the-way Victorian mining town. But perhaps the appellation "Switzerland of America" came before Ouray established itself as one of the premier high-country towns of America.

Cliffs and waterfalls mark the city limits of this village in the depths of the great San Juan mining region. Uncompahgre Canyon, with its hot and cold springs, mines, and chasms, is but five minutes from downtown. A little further down the road is Box Canyon, where a high bridge gives a good lookout at the falls thundering through the carved passage.

Ouray's San Juan Odyssey _____

*5th Ave. and Main St. Nightly 8:30 P.M. showing.
325-4607.*

☐ The Old Opera House is a fine setting for
this show, which is a great calling card to
introduce Ouray. Five screens and fifteen pro-
jectors do a good job of capturing the mountain
glory in a thirty-five-minute presentation.

Ouray Historical Museum _____
5th St. and 6th Ave.

☐ The three-floor museum, housed in an 1887
hospital, gives a historical background. The
reconstructed general store, bedroom, and dental
office indicate bits and pieces of life in Ouray
in the glory days, when the population reached
3000 (about 700 now call the town home).

A 1902 booklet describes this gem of a town:
"Good hotels, all modern conveniences, two
dollars to four dollars per day; lower rates by
the week. Connected with Denver and all
principal places by telephone. Horses, burros,
carriages, and guides to all places of interest at
reasonable rates."

Jeeping in Ouray _____

☐ Horses still wind their way through forested
paths, but jeeps have replaced the carriages and
burros in this "Jeeping Capital of the World,"
where more four-wheel drive vehicles are owned
per capita than anywhere in the U.S. Jeep
rentals for either half or full days are plentiful,
or join one of several organized four-wheel tours.

Jeep trails climb to the tundra on Engineer
Mountain and pass grassy basins with views to
Mt. Sneffels and Mt. Potosi. Old ghost towns of

Sneffels, Uradius, and Camp Bird are all within a half day's drive.

Hot Springs Mineral Pool_____

☐ At the end of a bone-jarring day's drive, the Hot Springs Mineral Pool at the north end of town gives soothing relief. It's open daily in summer except Mondays, and several days a week in winter. That's when locals say is the best time to enjoy the area's hot springs, as the town is quiet, the mountains white, the air crisp, and the water hot.

TELLURIDE

Butch Cassidy stormed through in 1889, robbing his first bank. It still stands on the east side of Main Street, near the chunky pink elephant painted by Hollywood when the movie was filmed. The elephant is picturesque, as is the "bath" sign across the street, but neither were necessary for authenticity or charm. Telluride already had more than its share.

Willie Nelson called it the most beautiful place he'd ever seen. Dizzie Gillespie went further: "If this isn't paradise, then heaven can wait."

Telluride Mountain Village. But visiting this remote, end-of-the-road valley can't wait, since the ski mountain is being transformed into a mountain village for 7000 visitors. Herds of elk graze on the golf course, and dense aspen groves have been flattened for the gigantic parking lot where visitors will leave their cars to ride the gondola into town.

Give this remote village a few years before expecting to find big name tennis tournaments, paved biking trails, luxurious exercise clubs, and fast-food outlets. Look instead for some of the best four-wheel drives in the state, and back country hikes that begin two blocks from the friendly downtown.

Telluride Hiking. Because the village is nearly surrounded by mountains, many trails begin right in town. Most popular of these is Bear Creek Canyon Trail. Take the Bear Creek Road at the end of South Pine Street, and follow it two miles to the falls. Another trail beginning in town is the Cornet Creek Trail. Go north from Aspen Street for about half an hour to reach Cornet Waterfall. To reach Savage Basin and Tomboy Ruins, walk about two-and-a-half hours north from Oak Street.

The trickling falls seen from town are Ingram Falls. Driving or walking towards them, Bridalveil Falls become visible. It's the state's highest waterfall drop, and the water's velocity is so great that it's impossible to stand close.

Telluride Jeeping. This is the place to forget your aversion to dust, rutted roads, and steep drop-offs. Even passenger cars can reach many out-of-the-way spots, such as Lizard Head Pass and the old mining town of Alta, with its two-story boarding house. Jeeps are a must for Imogene and Ophir passes. The Imogene road climbs roughly to a spectacular 13,114-foot pass on its way to Ouray. The Ophir trip begins at Old Ophir and comes out on Red Mountain Pass, about five miles north of Silverton.

Telluride Festivals. Telluride calls itself the festival capital of Colorado and it lives up to the name beginning in late May with the Mountain Film Festival and ending with the Hang Gliding Festival in September. In between is the Dance Festival and Workshop, a weekend of big names in jazz, and the Bluegrass and Country Music Festival, one of the biggest musical events in the West.

Montrose

Ute Indian Museum _____

South of Montrose on Highway 789. Monday-Saturday, 10–5; Sundays 1–5.

☐ This beautiful little museum is special because it's the only museum dedicated to just one tribe.

The white man's good ally, Chief Ouray, is the museum's focus. He was the famous Southern Ute Indian chief who, along with his successor Buckskin Charlie, steered a course of moderation and compliance. Despite a willingness to compromise, the Utes were herded off their western slope lands to Utah and southern Colorado.

Chief Ouray and his wife Chipeta traveled the United States in search of justice for their nation. Chipeta became a hit in white Eastern society, as she never forsook her Indian dress. Photos show her years after Ouray's death, wrapped in a ragged blanket and living with her people.

Backroads of Colorado

by Boyd and Barbara Norton

The Boyds have absorbed Colorado at a
leisurely pace and at close range. In the
process they've come up with forty mini-tours
to lure drivers from the expressway to hidden
valleys, alpine lakes, and forgotten towns. Each
drive is narrated in a folksy way, which makes
the reading almost as good as the driving.
   Every backroad tour provides directions, as
well as descriptions of the area
and its history.

CHAPTER 2

WEST CENTRAL

CRESTED BUTTE
GUNNISON
ASPEN
SNOWMASS
GLENWOOD SPRINGS
GRAND JUNCTION

CRESTED BUTTE

For years, Crested Butte was one of those little mountain towns that was too special to die. At the end of a dead-end road, snuggled high in the Elk Mountains, it attracted its aficionados who enjoyed the superb fishing, hiking, and snow of Gunnison Country.

With commercial airlines now landing in Gunnison and a highly rated golf course at the southern city limits, Crested Butte has left its sleepy past for the fast lane of the major resorts. Mt. Crested Butte, at the base of the ski mountain, is a maze of condominiums overshadowed by a large hotel.

But a mantle of faded Victorian authenticity rests upon the town. As a National Historic District, its buildings are somewhat protected from the tawdriness that envelopes many tourist spots sooner or later. The miniature wooden stores with their whimsically painted eaves invite leisurely browsing and picture taking.

A pamphlet lists forty-two sites to visit, surely enough to walk off the calories from The Bakery Café's pastries. The tour highlights include the amazing (a two-story outhouse), the picturesque (Union Congregational Church), the mundane (you decide for yourself), and the authentic (Kochevar Home of the 1880s).

Quaint as the town is, Crested Butte's attraction is beyond the city limits. Consider the four-and-a-half-mile trek to Green Lake, a ride up the Silver Queen Chairlift followed by a hike to the summit, or rafting the gentle Gunnison River. Flowers are at their height in July, coinciding with the Wildflower Festival, a one-week workshop in natural history, photography, and landscaping.

Mountain bikes are appreciated here more than anywhere else in the Rockies. Choose your level of adventure, from a maintained road to an overgrown miner's trail. The climax comes in September, when the Fat Tire Bike Week brings together industry reps, competitors, and recreational riders for the nation's largest gathering of this thigh-burning sport. Hundreds of them strap on helmets for the Pearl Pass Tour, a rutted and rocky shortcut to Aspen.

Gothic

☐ A little farther north, the former ghost town of Gothic nestles 9470 feet high in one of Colorado's most beautiful mountain valleys. One hundred years ago, this aerie's serenity was challenged by miners who turned it into the country's largest and wildest camp. Population soared into the thousands, then dropped just as suddenly. For over thirty years, the town's last mayor, Garwood Judd, was its only resident.

Gothic is now a private town, owned by the Rocky Mountain Biological Laboratory, so travel off Main Street is restricted. But north of town are two campgrounds and a picnic area.

Kebler Pass

☐ Kebler Pass, which follows an old Ute trail running between West Elk Wilderness and Ruby Range, is the quickest route from Aspen to Crested Butte. The highlight on Kebler can be the sheep, which Nike-clad shepherds herd in flocks of 2000 (all white except for three legendary blacks). Bleating, baaing, and roughly nursing on the graveled trail, some convene in groups of about twenty, heads together, oblivious of the passing jeep, while others foolishly dart

inches in front of the bumper, acting on a mis-
guided whim to join their friends.

Miners riddled this aspen-forested drive with
their tunnels. Seven miles out from Crested
Butte, at the shore of Lake Irwin, is a cemetery,
the only evidence of a once-thriving town that
in 1882 boasted three churches, six sawmills,
and two busy marshals who usually kept the jail
full. The miners were obviously not there just
for the views of Ruby Range; within three years
they had all left, following new rumors of riches.

GUNNISON

Tumbling down from massive peaks, such as
14,309-foot Uncompahgre, are more than 2000
miles of prime fishing streams. The shoreline of
Blue Mesa laps along 96 miles, making it Colorado's longest lake. This is fisherfolks heaven,
no doubt about it.

Everything in Gunnison Country is done on a
grand scale:

- Captain John Gunnison, who left his name
  on the valley in 1853 while surveying for a
  railroad, died in a Utah Indian attack from
  not one, but fourteen, arrows.
- The world-record elk head was bagged
  here and hangs in dusty glory in a hard-
  ware store.
- Rancher (and eventually governor) Dan
  Thornton raised Colorado's first two
  $50,000 Hereford bulls and displayed them,
  not in a stock show, but in the lobby of the
  Brown Palace Hotel.
- The mid-July Cattlemen's Days Rodeo is
  the oldest in Colorado.
- The county has been rated as one of the "best
  100" counties in America in which to live.

Jeeping. There are weeks of jeep trails to follow into National Forest lands, all of which pass enticing ghost towns whose names alone are enough to lure the curious over miles of brain-shattering ruts. Cumberland Pass takes off from Pitkin, passing the remnants of the Bon Ton and Blistered Horn Mines before reaching Tincup. At 12,200 feet, the pass is the highest standard-car road open in the summer.

If wide and gentle Monarch Pass keeps Texans shivering in their boots all the way home, consider Old Monarch Pass. From Sargents, head north up Tomichi Creek six miles to a sign that says "No Name Creek," then continue four miles along the Tomichi to the old mining town of Whitepine. In the days before fuel pumps, the steep grade forced drivers to back up for the entire climb to feed gas to their engines.

Cochetopa Pass (pass of the buffalo), off Colorado 114, was much used by the Ute Indians, since it is the easiest crossing of the Continental Divide in Colorado. The pioneers transformed it into the central route to the Pacific.

Cycling. Fat tire bikes go everywhere the jeeps do. Directly across from the Gunnison Chamber of Commerce is one of the finest bike tracks in the country. The premier racers converge in mid-September for Crested Butte's Fat Tire Bike Week, which includes a rough ride over Pearl Pass to Aspen.

Curecanti National Recreational Area___

Includes three lakes, beginning with Blue Mesa Lake, sixteen miles west of Gunnison along U.S. 50.

□ No one knows if the wily fifteen-pound Geronimo still lurks in Blue Mesa Lake with its ninety-six-mile shoreline. His legendary size grew with everyone who snagged and then lost him.

Blue Mesa Lake and its two sister bodies of water, Morrow Point Lake and Crystal Lake, are part of the Curecanti National Recreation Area. Boating, water skiing, sailing, and wind surfing are now possible because the Upper Colorado River Storage Project flooded miles of the famous Gunnison River.

The best way to get a first-hand look at the river-that-used-to-be is with Morrow Point Black Canyon Boat Tours (641-0402). A cabin cruiser skims along the steep canyon walls, hugging the shoreline where tracks of the Rio Grande Railroad once ran.

The Curecanti Creek Trail (five miles west of Blue Mesa Dam on Highway 92) descends one thousand feet along the creek to Morrow Point Lake and ascends a grueling one thousand feet back up. Standing astride one of two foot bridges, you'll see the river flowing turbulently underneath and minute bits of ground stone scouring the rocks, trying to carve the canyon ever deeper.

Black Canyon of the Gunnison _____

Follow U.S. 50 west from Gunnison for fifty-seven miles, turn at Colo. 347, the monument entry.

☐ Like the Na Pali cliffs on Kauai, the Black Canyon is one of those places where having a bird brain would be an advantage. Peer like the great horned owl into the somber depths. Soar like a sparrow hawk next to the sheer cliffs. Glide silently like a golden eagle through the turbulent chasm.

For those traveling without wings, or ropes and pitons, vistas are limited to the handrail-bound viewing ledges along the north and south rims.

A little geology is in order. In the Gunnison's

hurry to join the Colorado, it falls about ninety-five feet a mile. This drop is about three times steeper than the Colorado River's fall through the Grand Canyon. Since the water runs downward so swiftly, almost all the scouring action takes place on the river bottom and very little on the sides. That explains why the Black Canyon combines depth, narrowness, and sheerness.

The three upstream dams have considerably tamed the river, but its carving action, dramatic though the results are, was never much to notice. Since the tumbling boulders and silt began their first tentative scrapings, they have dug approximately the depth of two hairs every year. Who ever said that persistence doesn't have its rewards?

The visitors' center is the place to find out about nature walks, Sunday climbing demonstrations, and nightly campfire programs. Trails of a few feet to 1.4 miles round trip lead to the rim. The views are spectacular, but the ages are unbelievable. The underlying rock on the first overlook, for example, is 1.1 billion years old. It was once part of the roots of an ancient mountain range which has been uplifted. The dark rocks in the gorge are closer to 2 billion years old. Numbers like that are as difficult to comprehend as the canyon's very existence.

ASPEN

If the town's 1879 name hadn't been changed, Ute would be one of the world's most famous ski resorts. The Ute name was short-lived, perhaps because it was a too obvious reminder that the land of the Roaring Fork Valley had legally belonged to the Indians.

Aspen was one of the biggest silver towns in the West. Within months after its fantastic riches were discovered, 100-pound balls of ore, wrapped in cowhide, were being rolled down the sides of Aspen and Smuggler mountains and loaded on mule trains to Leadville.

Speaking of Culture

Wheeler Opera House. New York industrialist Jerome B. Wheeler developed an interest in Aspen, buying up mines and building a smelter at the junction of the Roaring Fork River and Castle Creek. By 1892, two of Aspen's landmark buildings had been completed and named after Wheeler: the Hotel Jerome and Wheeler Opera House.

The red hues of the lavish Opera House with its elaborately curtained corner boxes glitter once more under the massive central chandelier. A weeknight series of chamber music concerts is held in the intimate setting during the summer, as well as many performances throughout the year.

Aspen Music Festival. The Aspen Music Festival has thrived every summer since 1949 under some of the most inspired music directors of our time. Each year, accomplished artists and exceptionally talented students present more than 150 concerts encompassing nearly every musical genre and time period.

Aspen is a very special place to make music, with its superlative setting, nineteenth-century charm, and enthusiastically supportive community. A former student explains: "There is no place else like Aspen. It is a testing ground for us, one where we can experience a total immersion in music. We come for that, and not only to play under, but with, some of the finest professional artists anywhere."

The renowned festival begins in late June
and runs through late August. Initially the concerts were held in every available space throughout town. Now 80,000 visitors hear performances
primarily in the Saarinen-designed music tent
and the Victorian Opera House.

Afternoon concerts at 4:00 make Sundays
special. Many people bring picnics and feast on
the lawn before the symphony orchestra arrives.

The Ballet/Aspen Festival. The Ballet/
Aspen Festival, the largest ballet festival west of
the Mississippi, begins in July and runs for over
a month, with performances by some of the
country's outstanding companies and stars.

Aspen Art Museum. Overlooking the
Roaring Fork River, The Aspen Art Museum
offers a full summer schedule of exhibitions.
Guided tours are held every Wednesday at
12:30 and Thursday evening at 6:00. The evening
tour is part of the complimentary wine and cheese
reception held Thursdays from 5:30 to 7:00.

Walking Aspen's Victorian Streets _____

□ Downtown Aspen keeps browsers occupied
for days. As in Boulder, Aspen's pedestrian
malls invite relaxed enjoyment. Winding streams,
splashing fountains, and dense landscaping
almost eliminate views of the shops and encourage people-watching and patio-dining. Street
musicians hold court afternoons and evenings.

The West End is the residential area of
Victorian homes of the 1890s mining barons.
Whether it is seen on foot or by bicycle, the
neighborhood has a substantial charm that isn't
duplicated in any other Colorado mining town.

Wheeler-Stallard House Museum. 620
W. Bleeker. 925-3721. Summer and winter, 1–4.

The Wheeler-Stallard House was built in 1888
by the same Mr. Wheeler responsible for the
hotel and the opera house. The home is packed
with furniture, photos, and collections from
many area homes.

Aspen's reputation as a laid-back community
began decades ago. Photos in the carpeted
carriage house reveal that the Colorado Midland
Railroad, loaded with ore and Denver-bound
passengers, would oblige tourists by stopping at
likely looking fishing holes.

Heading for the Hills

☐ The first hill that most head to is Maroon
Bells. Like Bear Lake in Rocky Mountain Park,
the trailhead was being loved to death by
motorists. Now, from 9 to 5 in the summer a
special bus plies the Maroon Creek Road,
depositing hikers, photographers, fisherfolks,
and picnickers.

The three mountains of the Maroon Bells are
so majestic and so perfectly framed by the
valley that even Instamatic photographers get
inspired to shoot. The one-and-a-half-mile round-
trip trail to Beaver Lake follows and crosses a
tumbling creek. Nimble hummingbirds dart
among the aspen, while fat marmots placidly
continue their sunbathing routine. Two-hour
nature walks are led daily by naturalists from
Hallam Lake. Nominal fee.

When skiers first saw Mt. Hayden, towering
above Ashcroft Valley, they were ready to fell
trees, build a tram, and print brochures. But
World War II intervened, and by the time the
smoke cleared, Aspen Mountain became the
site of the ski hill, not Mt. Hayden.

Today's hikers and cross-country skiers reap
the benefits of the changed plans, since the

valley is as beautiful now as then, with nary a condo in sight. One-and-a-half miles from the base of the Elk Mountains, Ashcroft is head-quarters for cross-country ski trails that take off for destinations as ambitious as Pearl Pass or as tame as Pine Creek Cookhouse, which serves some of the tastiest meals in Pitkin County.

In 1987, the Silver Queen Gondola opened Aspen Mountain to the summer. The thirteen-minute ride to the 11,212-foot summit shaved hours off of what had been an excruciating uphill struggle.

The ride costs dearly. But the trade off is a day of wildflowers, hikes, a wiener doused with sauerkraut from the Sundeck Restaurant, and see-forever views of the Elk Mountain Range. Guided walks, led by naturalists from Hallam Lake, leave from the summit at 11 and 1.

T Lazy 7 Ranch (925-7254) has been a tra-dition for decades. Rustic accommodations, sleigh rides, horseback riding in the summer, and Wednesday and Thursday evening barbeques and foot-stomping to country music keep every-one coming back for more.

One of the few places in Aspen where snow-mobiles can be rented, T Lazy 7 revs them up by the dozens. Guides are unnecessary, as miles of well-marked trails surround the ranch. A one-hour ride leads to Maroon Lake, inaccessible by car in winter.

Ghost towns. The Castle Creek Road, which veers left at the Prince of Peace Chapel west of Aspen, heads to Ashcroft, a deserted mining town that once had a population of 5000. The hotel still stands firm against the hard alpine weather, as do several stores and cabins, thanks to the restorative efforts of the Aspen Historical Society.

The womenfolk had a penchant for planting gooseberry and rhubarb by their doorsteps. Often the still-thriving shrubs are the only evidence of a former home. Other cabin sites are defined by cellar pits that had been dug under the home to store vegetables.

The eerie déjà vu experienced while walking the grassy streets between the brown plank homes and stores is traceable not to a former life as an 1880s grubstaker but to an addiction to 1950s television, when the Lone Ranger and Tonto frequented Ashcroft.

Independence, near the eastern entrance to Aspen, is another true ghost town that rewards a thorough exploration.

Aspen Center for Environmental Studies. (Hallam Lake) 100 East Puppy Smith Rd. 925-5756. This center helps make the outdoors accessible to children and their parents.

Summertime Wildlife Expeditions are held for eight- to twelve-year-olds Monday, Wednesday, and Friday afternoons from 12 to 5. For $15, children are taken on adventures throughout the Aspen area.

Tuesdays and Thursdays, children from three to seven have their turn. An hour of outdoor programs precedes a noon picnic with their families. The center also holds walks for families, tours of the nature preserve, morning bird walks, and other adult programs.

When a mantle of snow covers all the familiar landmarks, two-hour snowshoe walks are held daily. Just a five-minute walk from town, Hallam Lake is a watering hole for ducks, Canadian geese, a golden eagle, racoons, a fox, a falcon, and an owl.

Snowmass

Hard bed rolls, stiff hiking boots, full can- teens, and too-heavy backpacks are no longer requisites for mountain vacations. In fact, the majority of Colorado's high-country visitors never get on a mountain trail (!). Snowmass Village is one of those places where so much is going on that hiking becomes just one of a hundred options.

Close to Aspen, but far enough away to have its own identity, Snowmass Village has become, for many families, the first vacation choice in the Elk Range.

With most lodges perched on the hillside, the serenity and challenges of the mountains are just outside the door. Festivities are ever- present, and cultural events are more extensive than those found in many large cities. The Guest Services Office (one level below the Mall,

beside the main pool, 923-2000) and the Information Booth in the Village Mall have information about all these events and more.

Snowmass Repertory Theatre. With
over 3000 applicants for a handful of positions,
director Michael Yeager chooses from the cream
of the actor's crop. Winter and summer performances from SRT, one of only two professional
repertory companies in Colorado, have earned
them top-notch reviews since their 1985 debut.

Horseback riding. Pioneer Springs Ranch
and Snowmass Stables are on the road into
town. With such innocuous names as Sam and
Henry, the steeds can be relied on for gentle,
almost bounce-free excursions. The breakfast
ride at Snowmass Stables often draws more
than fifty guests, and the evening barbecue is
even more popular.

Don't equate "trail breakfast" with "rustic
mountain meal served on a log." Several chefs
present a gourmet buffet, complete with fresh
flowers. With a choice of Danish, meats, eggs,
and platters of fruit, the highlight here is
definitely breakfast, not the twenty-minute ride.

Snowmass Stables' breakfast and dinner
rides lead up a hill to a valley overlook.
Children congregate at a stone-rimmed pond by
the picnic tables, where ravenous ten-inch trout
oblige these novice fisherkids.

Hot-air ballooning. The village's most
colorful festival takes place in July, when more
than forty brilliant balloons float through the
valley in the world's highest balloon race. It's
the only weekend when most alarms are set for
5:00 A.M.: the lift-off is at 6:00, to take
advantage of the early morning calm.

Year-round, four balloons are available for flights over the mountains. Service includes complimentary champagne to toast a successful flight.

Nature hikes. Frequent and free guided nature hikes, available through the Information Booth, are a painless way to bone up on the flora, fauna, geology, and history of the Roaring Fork Valley.

In the winter, these walks become snowshoe tours. The three-hour adventure departs in the morning, and a small fee covers equipment and instruction. As the group awkwardly treks its way through the valley, the naturalist points out wintertime plant and animal adaptations, animal tracks, and other sights that most would miss as they concentrated on getting one foot in front of the other.

Children's programs. Snowmass Pioneers enjoy hiking. Horseback riding. Field trips. Swimming. Picnicking. All these activities, plus games and crafts, are designed to bring participants closer to their mountain environment.

Too bad the program is only for children five to ten years old, as it sounds therapeutic for all ages. The day-care operates from 9–4, with daily or weekly registration.

The Snowmass Ski School Teen Program is one of a kind. Teenagers' energy levels are usually off the Richter scale: a day of hard skiing is just a warmup to them. The Snowmass program begins when the lifts open and ends long after sundown. The emphasis each day is teaching ski techniques, but once the lifts close, the teens keep going with cross-country skiing, sledding down Fanny Hill, softball games on skis, ski films, and sleigh rides. All events are supervised by ski school volunteers.

Aspen/Snowmass Nordic Council_____

☐ As if four mountains weren't enough, a fifth
ski area connects Snowmass, Buttermilk, and
Aspen. As North America's most extensive network of groomed and backcountry cross-country
trails, it's an exhilarating—and free—option to
downhill.

The forty-eight-mile system is consolidated
in an area of fifteen miles, accessible from nearly
anywhere in the Aspen/Snowmass valley. Get
acclimatized on the flat terrain of the Aspen Golf
Course; add the scenery of the Rio Grande
Trail that follows the Roaring Fork River along
an old railroad corridor. Moderate challenges
await at the Aspen Club and the Snowmass
Club Trails.

When your technique is down pat, and your
lungs are no longer homesick for lower altitudes,
you're ready for Owl Creek Trail, the crowning
jewel of the network. It begins at the Butter-
milk/Tiehack parking lot and leads into what
may be the most exhilarating corridor in the
Rockies before tying into Snowmass Club trails.
After the seven-mile one-way ski, there's the
option of taking a shuttle back.

Hut to Hut Skiing_____

☐ For the expert cross-country skier, limitless
unmaintained touring trails fan out from Aspen.
In the venerable European tradition, huts are a
warm and dry alternative to snow caves. To the
south, the Alfred Braun Memorial Huts perch
above Ashcroft. Beyond these, Friends' Hut is
over the crest of Pearl Pass. To the northeast,
the Tenth Mountain Trails Association is devel-
oping a hut network stretching from Aspen to
Vail. Four are now in place.

Call early for reservations and prepayment for any of the huts; weekends fill up as soon as the snow falls.

Krabloonik Kennel Tours and Dog Sledding

Straight up Brush Creek Road, near top of Snowmass Village. Dog sled rides, 923-4342. Restaurant, 923-3953.

☐ In the filtered shade of an aspen grove, more than 150 sled dogs sprawl, sleep, and watch the world go by, often from the roof of their individual dog houses. Their summer rest is well earned, as they work all winter pulling sleds through the Snowmass hills.

These hybrids of Malamute, Eskimo, and Siberian are descendants of dogs used in the 19th Mountain Division during World War II and later raised for sledding by the Toklat kennels.

In winter, the hand-fashioned sleds mush their way through deep snows, carrying no more than two adults and one child. It's an expensive experience, but an authentic one, and Krabloonik is the world's largest sledding operation.

GLENWOOD SPRINGS

Glenwood Hot Springs and Vapor Caves

9–9 daily except Thanksgiving and Christmas. Pool is also closed one day a month for cleaning. 945-5825.

☐ Where's the key to success? It used to be hidden in the scalding waters of Yampah Spring.

Native American warriors on their way up, and those hoping to stay on top, ritually bathed in the natural caves of Glenwood Springs. Legend has it that once they breathed the steam from the 115-degree water, they left as better hunters and mightier warriors.

In some homes, a shower or two is all it takes to empty the hot water tank. So how big must a natural spring be to heat the world's largest open-air pool, one that stretches two city blocks? The spring's water is so hot that it is mixed with cooler water before being emptied into the enormous swimming hole.

The massive children's wading area is as large as most public pools. Next to it, a 104-degree therapeutic pool simmers away all cares.

GRAND JUNCTION

Colorado National Monument _____

Access is from Grand Junction or Fruita on Colo. 340 to Rim Rock Drive. A thirty-six-mile circuit can be made from either city.

☐ The yin and yang of the geologic world ensures that every mountain that rises will ultimately give itself up to the forces of erosion, grain by grain. You don't have to hurry to catch this canyon's drama: it began 350 million years ago, and no end is in sight.

The black bench of rock that underlies the cliffs is more than a billion years old. This somber inner core of Precambrian rock is ten times older than the canyon's red cliffs. It was deposited when life was just beginning in warm ocean waters.

Mother Nature has been diligent over the eons in sculpting the reddened landscape. She rewards those who also take time. Settle on a ledge to listen to the silence. Watch for a canyon wren flitting through the mountain mahogany. Experience the textures and gradations of time-worn sediments. Descend the Liberty Cap Trail to become one with this ancient land.

A full canteen makes off-pavement exploration

possible in the summer. Winter cross-country
trips follow well-worn deer trails throughout
the canyon. Author Stephen Trimble, who has
written so beautifully of the monument, chooses
Ute Canyon as his favorite for walking and
photographing. At the head of the canyon, spring
runoff has gouged a series of potholes whose
waters delicately reflect the canyon's colors.
Surrounding the pools grow the canyon's only
trees: large, broad cottonwoods.

Rim of Time

by Stephen Trimble

A thirty-two-page booklet parading the awe-
inspiring beauty of Colorado National
Monument, along with a generous dash of its
geologic and human history. Trimble encourages
readers to see the magnificent vistas, as well as
to focus carefully on the canyonlands as a
sanctuary—albeit a harsh one—for
flowers, pinons, junipers, and
wildlife.

CHAPTER 3

NORTHWEST

COLORADO-UTAH BORDER
STEAMBOAT SPRINGS
ESTES PARK

Colorado-Utah Border

Dinosaur National Monument _____

Straddles the northern Colorado-Utah border. Visitors'
center, seven miles north of Jensen, Utah, is the only
place in the park to see dinosaur bones. Open daily
except Christmas, New Year's, and Thanksgiving.

☐ Just what should a dinosaur park have? The
ones in Rapid City and Calgary display vividly
painted models of the fabulous reptiles, looking
like poorly done stand-ins for a low-budget
B-movie.

Visitors to Colorado's remote park drive
hundreds of miles to view a window on the
Morrison. That's right. It's not exotic, but it's
the real thing.

Let's go back to the midpoint of the Age of
Dinosaurs, during a geologic time known as the
Morrison. Northwestern Colorado was a low-
lying plain crossed by meandering rivers and
streams, abundant with greenery. Stegosaurus,
with his two rows of teeth, loved it here, as did
the horny-beaked Dryosaurus. They and their
relatives chomped on the conifers and occasion-
ally on each other. They lived and died, largely
without leaving a trace.

Some died near a river. During heavy rains,
the overflowing waters would pick them up and
wash them downstream, along with turtles,
crocodiles, and tons of sand and gravel. They
were carried until they got stuck on a bank or a
sandbar. The present-day quarry in remote
Utah was such a sandbar.

Thousands of bones were excavated from
this site since its discovery in 1908 by a paleon-
tologist. What's left forms one wall of the
quarry. During the summer, technicians work

further on exposing the bones, but none are
now removed from this site.

After visiting the visitors' center and the
quarry, there's not much left to do in the upper
level of the park, other than take moderate
walks. Longer hikes are difficult because of the
rugged terrain and absence of drinking water.
The shortest, easiest trail is the Plug Hat Trail,
four miles north of headquarters. Exhibits
describe local history and geology.

Two-mile Harpers Corner Trail is the most
scenic, and pinyons and junipers make at least
a little shade during rest stops. The trail follows
a sunbaked ridge that allows great views of the
Green and Yampa rivers, as well as of Echo
Park, 2500 feet below. Rafting is the only way
to get a whitewater view of the canyons, and
the rangers have information on the various trips.

STEAMBOAT SPRINGS

This is Billy Kidd country. Land of sweeping
valleys, cowboy hats, fast skiing, and a Hot Air
Balloon Rodeo. Fishing? With three hundred
lakes and nine hundred miles of streams, every
fisherperson has a favorite casting spot.

Hot springs. Not to forget the 150 hot
springs dotting Yampa Valley. The easiest to
enjoy is Heart Springs, now part of the Steamboat Health and Recreation Association. This
downtown swimming pool, heated by natural
springs, is kept at 82 degrees; the smaller pool
next to it reaches nearly 100.

Five miles out of town, on Strawberry Park
Road, a rock-lined natural hot springs is open
for a $3.50 fee.

Steamboat was named for a springs that
made chug-a-chug sounds at a sharp bend of the

Yampa. A railway cut silenced the noise, but
hot mineral water still empties into the river.
This springs can be visited as part of a city
park at thirteenth and Lincoln.

Hiking. The most popular trail starts at
Fish Creek Falls, but begins by car at the inter-
section of U.S. 40 with Third Street. Go north
one block on Third to Oak, then follow signs.
The best time to view the two-hundred-foot drop
is in July, when the frothy torrent is at its peak.
A six-mile trail parallels Fish Creek all the way
to Long Lake, just below the Continental Divide.
Many hikers head for Mt. Zirkel and Flat Top
Wilderness areas.

Scenic drives. Do your own, or go on a
jeep tour to the old mining town of Hahn's
Peak, the Hot Springs, or Fish Creek Falls.

A rugged jeep road heads directly to stubby
Rabbit Ears, about three miles north of the pass
of the same name. Turn off U.S. 40 at the sign
for Dumont Lake. An old ladder simplifies the
actual ascent. Another good ride and hike from
the same turnoff is to Fishhook Lake, where
catching a small trout is almost guaranteed.

Flying. Steamboat Aviation takes scenic
flights over the entire northwest Colorado area.

Boating. At Steamboat Lake, there's sailing
and water skiing; for kayaking or tubing, there
are the Yampa and Elk rivers.

River rafting. The Colorado and Yampa
rivers are right here, and the big water of Utah
just a few hours away. White water trips for a
half day, all day, overnight, or full week are
available.

Hot-air balloon rides. There's a chance to
compete or just watch when balloonists from
the Rocky Mountain region gather in July for the
Hot Air Balloon Rodeo. Winter Carnival, the
second week of February, includes a combina-

tion hot-air balloon/ski race. Skis go along in the balloon, and when it lands, participants race cross-country to the finish line.

Several companies offer year-round daily champagne flights.

ESTES PARK

Estes is long lines of traffic beginning Memorial Day and continuing through Labor Day, scores of taffy and hard-rock candy "shoppes," T-shirt bazaars, souvenir stands, and the gateway city to Rocky Mountain National Park. There's no way to avoid it and, in fact, thousands enjoy it.

Dude ranches. There are many motels and campgrounds, as well as the venerable Stanley Hotel. A popular vacation, however, is staying at one of the many nearby dude ranches, such as Peaceful Valley Lodge, where guided horseback rides begin early in the day with a breakfast ride to a secluded spot overlooking St. Vrain Glacier and continue throughout the day. Even more popular are the scout tours, with four-wheel drives exploring gold and silver mining camps or the old Switzerland Trail.

Children have supervised programs consisting of riding, swimming, crafts, hikes, and nature lore. And everyone is invited to the nightly square dance.

The dude ranch option offers immersion in the tranquil beauty of the mountains, proximity to Rocky Mountain Park, yet distance from the congestion of Estes.

Rocky Mountain National Park _____

Two-and-a-half million acres straddle the Continental Divide west of Estes Park.

☐ Welcome to the high country and Colorado's most visited mountain park. You'll be surprised at how few roads traverse this immense area, but there's a reason. This park is set aside to preserve the magnificent wilderness, one third of which is above tree line.

The drive through the park is across Trail Ridge Road; the other option is Bear Lake, one of the few high-mountain basin lakes that can be reached by a paved road. Its attraction is so great that a shuttle bus is necessary to avoid traffic congestion. Many trails leave from Bear Lake, but the most popular walk is the half mile around the lake itself.

A feature of Rocky Mountain Park is the marked differences found with the changing elevation. At lower levels are Douglas fir, ponderosa pine and juniper, groves of aspen, and densely packed lodgepole pines.

At about 9000 feet are forests of Englemann spruce and subalpine fir. In the cool shade, breathtaking wildflowers flourish, particularly Colorado's famous columbine. At the upper fringes of this zone, the trees become thick, shortened, and twisted, struggling to survive the fierce winds and extreme cold.

At about 11,500 feet, trees disappear, and the miniature world of alpine tundra begins. Many of these same plants grow in the arctic, thousands of miles to the north.

Trail Ridge Road. It's America's highest through highway and makes every Top Ten of Scenic Drives. Yet it's open a scant five months of the year, as snow buries it from mid-October on.

The scenic drama actually begins in Loveland, at the entrance to Big Thompson Canyon.
The road follows the Big Thompson River to
its source at the Continental Divide. In the canyon, two lanes snake beside the churning river,
flanked by rock walls so high that sunlight
reaches the valley floor only at midday. Here
and there, there's room for a handful of Indian
curio shops, small lodges, and cider houses.
Best stopping place is Viestenz-Smith Mountain
Park, a well-kept grassy area of picnic tables,
barbeques, and two National Recreation trails.

The canyon ends as abruptly as it began,
opening to a view over Estes Valley and Long's
Peak. Following U.S. 34 through Estes leads to
the Fall River Station. Just yards past it, civilization gives way to dense forest. But before
there's time to drink in the fragrant pine scent,
signs post "Bighorn Crossing." Scores of the
park's 500 sheep make their way down the
Mummy Range to lick mineral-rich mud around
Sheep Lakes.

The highway's dramatic rise begins at Deer
Ridge Junction. Along the short forty miles of
Trail Ridge, life zones are traversed equivalent
to a round trip to the Arctic Circle.

Several overlooks, each one more spectacular,
line the route as it meanders over mountaintops.
For those who want to experience this rarified
atmosphere, thirty minutes on Tundra Trail is a
once-in-a-lifetime walk, even though the constant twenty m.p.h. wind results in a wind chill
of thirty-five degrees on the warmest of days.
The gravelled trail is there for a reason; one
misplaced footprint sets back a plant's growth
by a decade.

Trail Ridge Road crests at 12,813 feet, a
couple of curves before the Alpine Visitors Cen-

ter, the only place along the way to buy snacks.
Next stop is the eyrie at Medicine Bow Curve,
where views extend all the way to Wyoming's
Snowy Range. Follow the road through the park
all the way to Grand Lake, on the western side
of the Continental Divide, and the source of
the Colorado River.

Park activities and hikes. A park publication lists two pages of naturalist activities. All sound inviting. There's a Twilight Trek, Ghost Town Ramble, Buds and Blooms, Sprague Lake Photo Walk, and more than fifty others to choose from. All guided by experts and all free.

Start with a visit to the Moraine Park Visitor Center, which opens Memorial Day weekend. The building itself is worth the stop, as it was a private hunting lodge before the park's nationalization. Massive river-rock fireplaces and hand-

hewn log furniture make it a perfect place to escape a sudden summer squall.

A ranger is on hand to answer questions, and a good selection of inexpensive pamphlets and books on the park is available. One particularly to note is *Walks with Nature in Rocky Mountain National Park* by Kent and Donna Dannen. It introduces visitors to five short walks and the experiences with nature that they provide.

With more than 300 miles of trails available in Rocky Mountain Park, hiking is almost requisite to a visit. Drawing on the Dannen's familiarity with the park, here are a few suggestions for approaches to a family mountain walk.

Along the paved path to popular Nymph Lake from Bear Lake, look for the many birds. Nutcrackers and gray jays compete with one another and with humans for food. Another common jay is the blue-and-black Stellar's.

Even on the short walk from Bear Lake to Nymph Lake the trees will vary. Engelmann spruce and subalpine fir rim Bear Lake; happily chattering red squirrels are busy in this area. Closer to Nymph Lake, lodgepole pines become more common. These are the tall straight trees the Indians once used for tipi poles.

Donna Dannen's favorite ecosystem is the tundra, where humans are giants. The native tundra is a world in miniature, as the growing season is so short and the long winter so inhospitable to life. The Dannens refer to tundra plants as "pioneer heroes." A cluster of pink moss campion as big as a hand span could be as old as twenty-five years; the first five years of life it grows only half an inch. More than any-where else in the park, this is the place to stay on the path. A careless footstep could destroy decades of growth.

On the walk from Moraine Park to Fern Lake, look for signs of glaciation. Flowing glaciers reshaped narrow valleys into wide, U-shaped valleys. Even individual rocks were affected: they often were polished smooth by thousands of years of grinding ice.

Some aspen have long black marks on the trunks about six to eight feet up. Man's initial-carving mania isn't the only threat to aspen bark. Elk vertically strip aspen bark, a favorite winter food.

Rocky Mountain National Park is one of Colorado's most popular attractions. Hundreds scale Long's Peak, thousands camp, six hundred thousand hike, and nearly three million see the vistas. Find the approach that works for you, and then enjoy.

Never Summer Ranch. In the moose-viewing territory of Kawuneeche Valley, at the western end of Trail Ridge Road, Never Summer Ranch tells the story of early day dude ranching in the Rockies. Touring the ranch is free, and guides from the park service fill in the details.

The Fall River Road (unpaved to this day) opened the park up to travelers in 1920. Arriving by wagon, Model As, and Model Ts, guests at Never Summer Ranch came not to be pampered but to revel in the rugged West. They ate local fare of trout, deer, and grouse and not surprisingly, stayed for weeks on end.

Walks With Nature in
Rocky Mountain National Park

by Kent and Donna Dannen

Few know this park as do Kent and Donna, and none love it better. With their work as photographers, writers, and naturalists, its myriad trails and peaks are as familiar to them as their own backyard. In fact, the park and the Dannens are neighbors.

This sensitive guide chats about the camp-robbers, raucous nutcrackers, and brave water ouzels. It takes time to examine the bark of slow-growing ponderosas, and to look in the shade of lodgepole woods for fairy slipper, calypso, and spotted coralroot. Walking with the Dannens is special indeed.

CHAPTER 4

CENTRAL ROCKIES

WINTER PARK

Winter Park Ski Train _____

Runs Saturday and Sunday during ski season, leaving from Union Station in Denver at 17th and Wynkoop. Two-and-a-half hours one-way. Ticket information, 623-8497.

☐ The Rio Grande Railroad isn't given to frivolity. So who would believe that it runs a train to paradise?

After fifty years of hauling skiers to Winter Park, even the Pullman coaches themselves were partied out. They were retired in the 1988 ski season and replaced with fourteen newer cars holding 775 passengers. The nation's only train exclusively serving a ski area continues to make history; three first-class cars have been added, giving adults an escape hatch from the frivolity of the coach cars.

Unlike its Amtrak relatives, this train leaves on schedule. In fifty years of service, it's only cancelled five times.

The trip through thirty-one tunnels, including the ten-kilometer Moffat Tunnel, ends right at the lifts. Lift tickets don't sell for $1 as they did when Winter Park opened in 1940, but there's far more to choose from than the original half-mile tow.

GEORGETOWN

Hotel De Paris _____

Taos and 6th streets, Georgetown. Self-guided tour. Summer, daily. Winter, afternoons except Monday.

☐ The concept of mountain luxury was not invented by Vail developers. An enigmatic wanderer, Louis DuPuy, opened a fine restaurant and hotel in Georgetown in 1875, two years before the railroad reached the silver queen city.

This worthwhile tour showcases a comfortable view of life during Georgetown's boom years when 5000 people lived in the valley.

DuPuy featured an exotic menu of oysters (half-dozen raw for thirty-five cents), sirloin steak, and mutton chops, all complemented by a fine wine cellar. The dining room is exceptional, with a maple striped floor and heavily appliqued green and coral walls. The kitchen is incredible, with a huge central brick oven.

DuPuy, a bachelor, lived adjacent to the dining room. A large folding bed and armoire took up what little room his collection of 1500 books left.

Hamill House _____

Georgetown. 3rd and Argentine streets. Summer, Memorial Day through September 30, 9–5 daily. Winter, 12–4 P.M. Closed Monday and Tuesday.

☐ For those who enjoy historical home tours, the Hamill House was the town's most ambitious home. Between the home and the granite offices is a highly decorated privy, divided in half to allow for the separation of family and servants.

Georgetown Loop Railroad _____

Departs from Georgetown Terminal and Silver Plume Depot (Exits 228 or 226 on I-70, seventy miles west of Denver) between 10:15 and 4:30. Daily in summer. Train ride is one hour; highly recommended mine tour plus ride is two hours, fifteen minutes. Georgetown, 569-2403. Denver, 279-6101.

☐ At more than a half million dollars a mile, this better be a good ride.

It is. The Georgetown Loop Railroad and mine tour is the state's best look at its mining

and railroad heritage. The Loop twists and turns
through fourteen sharp curves, snaking its way
down Clear Creek Canyon. Just before Georgetown it actually doubles back on itself ninety-
five feet in the air at the high trestle, Devil's
Gate Bridge.

A century ago, the Loop was called the
Eighth Wonder of the World. It was completed
in 1884 as an extension of the Union Pacific to
carry ore, supplies, and passengers. When
mining declined after 1893, tourists took up the
slack, coming thousands of miles to ride "that
famous knot in the railroad." At the height of
its popularity, seven trainloads of picnickers a
day rode the aspen-lined route.

During the Depression the train stopped
running, and in 1939 the high trestle was sold
as scrap for $450. What a mistake. To rebuild
it, now at ninety-five feet above the canyon,
was a million-dollar project of the Colorado
Historical Society, made possible through a
Boettcher Foundation gift.

The rebuilding of the "railroad in the sky" has
been a twenty-five year, $3.35-million project of
the society, engaging the muscle, imagination,
and money of thousands of volunteers. Four
miles of narrow-gauge track was laid down the
steep two-mile canyon from Silver Plume to
Georgetown.

The engines burn oil, making this the clean-
est narrow-gauge ride in the state. It happens

this way: Oil is burned to fuel the fire to boil the water to produce the steam to power the steam engines. As the engineer explained, "All you have here is a big teakettle."

The Lebanon Mine _____

An optional extension of the Georgetown Loop Railroad trip. A one-hour guided walking tour of the Lebanon Silver Mine. Daily in summer. Last two trains of the day do not offer mine tours.

☐ The Georgetown Loop is a good ride, but it can become great by adding the mine tour. Mining is, after all, the reason for Georgetown and the train.

Georgetown miners spent five hard years trying to extract gold from silver-bearing rock. But once silver was discovered in 1864, the rush was on.

The lure of the mines becomes a dark, sodden ordeal once you're actually inside a mountain. The Lebanon Mine tour goes in 600 damp feet, directly under the stream of I-70 traffic. There's no need to worry about rotten timbers: AJAX rebuilt the beginning of the tunnel with strong timber, and the rest of the tunnel bores through stable granite.

As are all mines, this one is chilly, with the temperature a constant forty-six degrees. The coolness was a big problem for miners, since dynamite freezes at fifty-two degrees. A dynamite warmer, with each stick in its own compart-ment, was heated by a candle underneath. Keep-ing that candle lit was a powerful responsibility.

The mining routine was fairly straightforward. In the Lebanon, ten men worked each shift. At the end of a shift, dynamite would be blasted, and the mine cleared for two hours. The next shift would muck up. Dynamite, muck up. Dynamite, muck up.

The Lebanon Mine tour is more thorough than many others, since a reconstructed miners' changing room and mine manager's office are also visited.

IDAHO SPRINGS

Argo Gold Mill _____

Idaho Springs. April–October. Self-guided tour.

☐ The tour is more of a mill than of a mine, since the Argo was built in 1913 to concentrate precious metal from the ores of Gilpin and Clear Creek counties.

The ores were brought to the Argo via the famous Newhouse Tunnel. But when an underground lake flooded the Argo mine in 1943, the Argo Mill lost its primary ore source and was closed.

The stamp room is silent now, but in 1913 twenty 1,050-pound stamps pulverized the ores. At 120 six-foot drops per minute, workers were deaf within six months.

Highway to Mount Evans _____

Mount Evans exit off I-70 at Idaho Springs.

☐ Endure the hairpin turns. Hug the road around the bends where no railing protects against dropoffs that leave the timid breathless. Hang on over the rough spots where last year's frigid temperatures crinkled the pavement.

All twenty-eight miles of the drive from Idaho Springs are special, but best of all is the summit. Skittish bighorn sheep may be overlooking the parking lot, or almost tame mountain goats may let you approach to within a few yards.

Then there's the landscape, one of the only places below the Arctic Circle with Arctic tundra. Whereas most Colorado tundra is dry, Arctic tundra grows on top of permanently frozen ground. Water cannot drain, so it remains in ice-spotted pools on the surface.

Just up from the midway point at Echo Lake, the Mt. Goliath Nature Area allows close-up views of the oldest trees of all, tortured bristle-cone pines. Their twisted trunks do daily battle with the wind and wear their scars proudly: often the bark has been worn off by windblown ice and rock granules and the underlying wood polished smooth.

The Alpine Garden Trail leads from the nature area through 300 varieties of wildflowers. This area is also the home of deer, elk, and badgers. Chipmunks, of course, are omnipresent at all 18,952 of Colorado's picnic spots.

BLACK HAWK

Bobtail Gold Mine

Highway 279 in Black Hawk. Daily, May-September, 10–6.

☐ Bobtail oxen pulled ore carts out of this fabulously wealthy gold mine before they were usurped by mules. Mules cost $24 to replace; miners who would work for $3.50 a day were plentiful. After an accident, owners first asked, "Any mules killed?"

Tired donkeys now pull tourist-laden wagons 900 feet underground on a twenty-minute tour.

CENTRAL CITY

Teller House Hotel and Central City Opera House

Eureka St., Central City. Tours leave from the hotel daily 11–5.

☐ Central City is a greedy carnival town – the only one of Colorado's many mining towns that dares to charge for parking. In fact, finding a decent free spot without having to hike in from the rut-filled triangle of free parking above the city can be as tricky as finding an interesting souvenir among the glut of shops.

This small tourist mecca with a full-time population of fewer than 500 eclipsed Denver in importance during the gold rush. In 1872, Teller began construction on one of the best hotels west of the Mississippi. The hotel had to be special in order to attract a clientele that could afford the steep charge of $3 a night, including two meals. With its elaborate construction and $2 million in antiques, the hotel is still a marvel.

Everything about the hotel is grand. An oxen team struggled nine days to haul in the lobby desk from Denver. On its next trip, the load was even more precarious: a twelve-foot diamond-dust mirror.

The register of guests reads like an Americana *Who's Who*: Mae West, Lillian Gish, Helen Hayes, Douglas Fairbanks, Jr., and Mark Twain. One magnificent red bedroom is named for President Grant, as its richly carved bed was paid for by gold miners. They were attempting to gain his favor over the silver miners, who had paved the street in front of the hotel with silver bricks.

The lavish interior of the Opera House next door attracts sellout crowds each summer, just as it did when Sarah Bernhardt and Edwin Booth performed for audiences of the 1880s.

KEYSTONE

It's hard to believe Keystone has a history beyond the excellent corporate decision to build the resort in the first place. A quick historical tour proves otherwise.

Historical tour. Reservations through Keystone Resort Activities Center. 468-4130. Why is the tongue-twister "Sts. John" used throughout Keystone? Did Montezuma really conquer Colorado?

You can win the next "Mountain Trivia" game with stray facts garnered during a two-hour historical tour given by the resort every Tuesday at 10 A.M. throughout the summer. The guides have devoured the Summit County library and give a thorough tour.

The Keystone Village before THE Keystone was rather ordinary. In fact, four sawmill workers lived in a room smaller than a condominium's second bedroom in the resort down the lane.

The cook for this Swedish lumbering community had the largest home. He often sat on the sloping roof, surveying his enormous cabbage patch that stretched toward the Snake River, a mild stream that runs from up near Montezuma.

Montezuma, along with dozens of other nearby mining towns, supported Keystone's milling operations. Tourists visiting it can't help but pick up rocks, wondering if they contain gold. The early miners wondered the same thing, and the answer was "no." But there was silver, discovered serendipitously by miners who ran out of ammunition while hunting deer. They hand-fashioned some bullets out of what they thought was lead. Years later, they saw silver ore while working in Nevada and had an instant playback of those old bullets they'd made. The race was on.

Trails near Montezuma. Montezuma is now a popular trailhead, both for cross-country skiers and summer hikers who want to visit now-deserted towns and mines. The most gentle trail is up Peru Gulch four miles to the old Pennsylvania Mine. Across from Inn Montezuma, a path takes off to the ghost town of Sts. John. It's two miles to the smelter and a little farther to the old town. In the winter, go as far as the plow goes on Montezuma Road, then continue for about four miles on gradual uphill terrain, skiing through scenic Deer Creek Valley.

Keystone Lake. Life in Keystone Resort revolves around the lake, home of Colorado's happiest, fattest, and longest-living trout. In order to perpetuate this idyllic condition, Trout Chow is available at the Activity Center. In the winter, the lake becomes the world's largest outdoor, maintained ice rink.

Summer activities. If you're in a hurry, or very dubious, take a half-day raft trip down the Blue. A full-day trip down the Colorado River is for those who want a lot of relaxing with only a sprinkling of white water. The narrower Arkansas River offers more thrilling full-day white water adventures.

Boat on Keystone Lake by renting a paddleboat, kayak, or wing sailer.

Jump in an open-top jeep for a two-hour tour of Arapaho National Forest.

Saddle the old mare and hop on for a ride that lasts anywhere from one to seven hours. More than forty miles of trails follow the Snake River, lead into the forest, or traverse a ridge for views of Ten Mile Range. Or enjoy a deluxe, wrangler-style breakfast ride.

Burrow into the hay in a horsedrawn wagon, which makes an afternoon trip to Soda Creek Valley, with its relics of an old cattle ranch.

Night skiing. Three hundred high-pressure lights give Keystone the most extensive night skiing operation in the country. They illuminate 2340 vertical feet; the jolt of the frigid air is softened by rides in the enclosed gondola.

For those who can never get in enough runs, it's possible to ski from 8:30 A.M. until 10:00 P.M.

VAIL

Vail is a variation on the classic American success story. Twenty-five years ago the narrow valley along Gore Creek was home to sheep ranches and potato farms. Today, it's a key stop on the international ski circuit and a vibrant world-class resort, with Beverly Hills styles and prices.

The free, albeit muddy, parking lot was long since paved and toll gates installed. Bridge Street classics such as the old Red Lion, Donovan's, and now The Deli have closed to make room for yet more retailers. Isn't there any place where ten dollars buys what it used to? Emphatically, yes.

Places. One of the best values is at the Vail Nature Center, just east of the village. Every day throughout the summer there are several scheduled activities: many are free, and others, such as the twilight Beaver Pond Walk, cost $1 for families. The longest adult hike is four hours; family flower walks are considerably shorter.

Between Vail and LionsHead is the free Colorado Ski Museum. Its exhibits and films illustrate 150 years of Colorado's ski history. To learn more about Vail Valley itself, watch the free multimedia slide show that runs every half hour from 10:00 to 5:00 in the gondola building.

Near the museum is the beautifully designed public library. This is how libraries look in small towns with big budgets and good architects. There's a full selection of stereo cassettes, magazines, audio/visual equipment, as well as special programming.

Hiking and biking. Hiking trails leave from Bighorn, Booth Creek, Piney Creek, and the village itself. Vail Mountain's well-marked trails vary from half a mile to four-and-a-half. Start hiking from the bottom, and be rewarded with a free gondola ride down. Afternoon guided hikes are available several days a week from Eagle's Nest.

The bike path begins in West Vail, runs through town, skirts the golf course next to national forest land, goes through East Vail, and keeps on going up 10,666-foot Vail Pass. From there on, it's downhill to Copper Mountain. That's not the end. Head south, and the bike paths continue from Copper to Frisco, and from Frisco to Breckenridge.

Other sports. Vail's athletic fields, east on Vail Valley Drive, draw hundreds of spectators to watch formidable competitions of rugby, soccer, lacrosse, softball, and volleyball teams. There's no charge to bask in the mountain sunshine. If you'd rather be doing than watching, The Dobson Arena (across from the library and on the free bus route) offers public skating and equipment rentals.

Come to think of it, there's never been a single Vail visitor who's run out of things to do, even inexpensive ones. This is just the start of a listing that has infinite variations, summer or winter. No wonder the kids come to ski for a weekend and stay for a season.

BEAVER CREEK

This start-from-scratch luxury resort is ten miles west of Vail, in its own secluded valley. Its original oh-so-exclusive demeanor worked too well at keeping the crowds away. Lately it's been loosening its tie and rolling up its sleeves to have some fun.

Chairlift rides. As of press time, Centennial Express up to Spruce Saddle was the best bargain in the Rockies. While everyone else was making a mint on summer chairlift and gondola rides, Beaver Creek's was free. The barbeque from the mid-mountain is as good as they get, and the views toward Gore Range are even better.

Beaver Creek Stables. Hourly rides as well as lunch rides go to Beaver Lake, and breakfast and dinner rides go to Beano's Cabin, the West's fanciest log cabin.

LEADVILLE

Healy House and Dexter Cabin _____

910 Harrison, Leadville. Summers only. Monday-Saturday, 10–4:30; Sunday, 1–4:30. Forty-five-minute tours.

☐ The too-long tour starts with a surprise. The rough exterior of the 1878 Dexter cabin is a foil for a luxurious two-room interior.

It's a comfortable cabin, the kind often pictured when thinking of a mountain escape. The bathroom is complete with a zinc-lined bathtub. The furniture is richly polished, the decorations appropriately masculine, and the fireplace inviting.

Dexter, who used the home as a retreat from his family in Denver, knew enough about housekeeping to know that kitchens mean work. Being a man who liked his pleasures, his home had *no* kitchen.

The Healy House is seen through living history tours representing the year 1899. However, living history only works when the guides have immersed themselves in the time period, knowing what people of that age wore, ate, drank, earned, and enjoyed. Sadly, these details are missing, and the tour concentrates on artifacts rather than on the personalities behind them.

The boarders living on the home's third floor were teachers, earning $47.50 monthly and paying $30 of that for room and board. The three rooms shared by six women were so minute that folding beds were used.

The house is well-furnished and is home to thousands of period artifacts. An amusing series of three dessert plates was painted by an inspired artist who had never seen the West.

His rabbits bound hillsides in herds, while cowboys lasso buffalo and tie elk to trees. Nelly Healy's teaching certificate records her 100 percent grammar score and a 75 percent in arithmetic.

Fortress towers decorate the wallpaper border in the parlor. They represent Leadville's most fanciful enterprise, the Ice Palace of 1896.

Leadville had been in a recession since the late 1880s when silver prices had dropped, deep-rock mining costs had eroded profits, and underground lakes had flooded many mines. In an effort to bring people to their town, an enormous ice palace was begun in November 1895.

Its scale was so gigantic—covering more than five acres—that worldwide attention was attracted. Eighteen teams of horses hauled more than 180 tons of ice to the site where men worked around the clock, despite temperatures far below zero, for the January 3, 1896, opening.

The Colorado Press Club spent a day in revelry at the palace ice rink, ballrooms, and dining room, but not before they passed a resolution: "The Leadville Ice Palace is the most beautiful sight ever gazed upon by man."

Ice palaces, following the same principle that reduces snowmen to puddles, melt all too soon. At one point in the winter, Mr. Wood, who invested more than $20,000 of his own funds in the palace, spent another $5000 buying muslin to keep the chinook winds off. But by March 18 the paper reported: "[The palace] will soon live but a memory as in a child's fairy tale. It is planned that March 28 will be the last day of the few remaining activities. A wire fence will be constructed around the palace, and it shall be closed forever."

Tabor House

116 E. 5th St., Leadville. Summer, 9–5. Self-guided tours of fifteen to twenty minutes.

☐ The Tabor Triangle is far more memorable than the Tabor millions. This is the home that preceded the triangle and the money. Horace and Augusta Tabor, along with their fifteen-month-old baby, joined the Colorado gold rush in 1859. In Denver, Augusta was one of only twelve women. Her industry over the next eighteen years helped keep her family afloat as they moved from mining camp to mining camp.

The few thousand dollars that Horace made in mining near Oro City was used to open a general store where he and Augusta worked for the next fifteen years. The Tabors would grubstake miners, providing food and supplies in exchange for an ownership interest in anything the prospectors found. In 1878, two of the men whom the Tabors had grubstaked found the Little Pittsburgh, one of the richest mines in Leadville's history.

The year before, the Tabors had built a new home for themselves in Leadville. Before this home was built, Leadville had only log cabins. But the coziness of their two-bedroom home was exchanged two years later for a twenty-room Denver mansion directly across the street from the Brown Palace.

The Leadville Tabor home contains a few pieces of original Tabor furniture, such as their son's cradle, Horace's fireman's hat (he organized the city's brigade), and several pictures of the Tabors. Augusta would be properly horrified, but tourist requests have resulted in the hanging of pictures of the infamous second wife as well.

Tabor Opera House_____

*Main St., Leadville. Open summers through October 1,
except Saturday.*

☐ As soon as Horace Tabor's pockets were
lined with silver, he began a string of projects.
In less than two years, he built the Leadville
gas works and municipal water works, organized
the telephone system, founded the bank, and
contributed to the building of several churches,
a school, and a hospital.

With the Central City opera already in place,
Tabor envisioned his Leadville Opera House as
being Colorado's second great "palace of cul-
ture." Groundbreaking was August 1, and by
November 20 the three-story building with its
grand staircase was complete.

The excitement of opening night was somewhat dimmed when two outlaws were hung just
a block away. But the eight hundred ticket
holders made their way to the Opera House to
applaud both Augusta and Horace Tabor, sitting
in their richly carpeted and draped box seats,
and the state's favorite actor, Jack Langrishe.

Leadville was now not just a mining camp
but a respectable city offering cultural events.
It became an important stop on the "Silver Circuit" of the theatrical troupes that toured Colorado before rejoining the primary east-west rail
line out of Cheyenne. For the nine months
before the railroad came, entertainers arrived
by stage. One letter found by the opera house's
present owner, Evelyn Furman, suggests the
hazards: the writer's coach tipped over six
times on its way from Denver.

The scarlet plush of the iron opera chairs is
dingy and brown now; the bright frescoed walls
are yellow with stains; the balusters have long

ago lost their white and gold paint; the seventy-two gas jets that brilliantly illuminated the hall have been only partially replaced by dim light bulbs. But with Tabor's Denver Opera House now demolished, this one stands as a record of Leadville's better days, a time when hopes were as high as Leadville itself.

Matchless Mine

Leadville. 1¼ miles east on 7th and Road 3. Summer, 9–5. 486-0371.

☐ This is not a mine tour but a visit to the one-room shanty where Mrs. Baby Doe Tabor spent her final years.

The Matchless is famous not for the nearly $7 million taken out of it but for the role it played in the life of Horace Tabor's second wife, Baby Doe.

While she, Horace, and their daughters Lillie and Silver Dollar once lived in a million-dollar mansion with a hundred peacocks flaunting themselves in the front yard, they were bankrupt by 1895. Horace died a few years later, and Baby Doe spent the next thirty-six years in desperate litigation in order to hang on to the Matchless Mine, which Tabor had predicted would once again "make millions."

Seven years before her death, the mine went on the block at a sheriff's auction for $25.65 in unpaid taxes but was withdrawn when no bids were received. With the help of benefactors, Baby Doe hung on. She eventually moved to a tool cabin close to the hoist house and made the Matchless her last home.

The mine was worked after her 1935 death, but meager profits closed it for the last time. It fell into ruins and her cabin was vandalized.

The shanty isn't much, nor was it ever. But a
visit to the site puts the dramatic Tabor story
into a personal perspective.

BRECKENRIDGE

Ghost towns. Why is it that ghost towns
are more interesting than many of the small
towns one speeds through on the way to some-
where else? As all traces of the mundane aspects
of life disintegrate, the remaining weathered
shell can be invested with a life of its own. Our
imagination can repopulate the deserted town.

Breckenridge is the only remaining village of
the scores that flourished in the Blue River
Valley. As late as the 1950s, it too was occasion-
ally listed as a ghost town. Indeed, its shuttered
buildings, weathered homes, and abandoned
storefronts qualified it in a nonliteral way.

History becomes yours in a ghost town. An
easy one to reach is the Boreas Pass Station, on
top of the Divide. This was once the highest
railroad station in the country. Near timberline
on the same road is the 7:40 tipple, 1.8 miles
past Baker's Tank. The heavy beams of the tipple
identify the spot where ore was loaded onto the
rail cars. A road to the right of the tipple leads
to Dyersville, founded by Father Dyer, the
Snowshoe Itinerant. (Leave the car behind and
walk this one.)

Preston is more out-of-the-way. Travel one-
half mile east on Tiger Road, turning right at
County Road 300. Past the Jesse mill and
beaver ponds, you'll see on the right the place
where the side of the mountain was blown out
by placer mining. Chinese coolies had the tedious
job of picking through the gravel, looking for
gold. Up Gibson Hill is Preston, its buildings
tilted this way and that. It was never much of a

camp. The mill machinery from the Little Corporal is just one-quarter mile away, as is the cyanide-charred landscape.

Hiking. The Arapaho National Forest, which surrounds Breckenridge, is made for hiking. A good choice for families is Rainbow Lake. At the crest of a hill south of Frisco on Highway 9 is a sign marking the lake. It's a gentle mile walk, and once at the lake many other options exist.

Sapphire Point is an even easier hike, leading to a panoramic view of Summit County. Parking for the trail is at the high point on Swan Mountain Road.

FAIRPLAY

South Park City

May 15–October 15.

☐ South Park City has everything except good public relations. This unproclaimed gem, tucked away on a Fairplay side street, is a three-star detour. All the billboards, full-color fliers, ads, coupons, and promotions that entice us to more dubious attractions are absent. As a result, South Park City's virtues go largely unsung.

What we have here is the Rocky Mountain area's most extensive collection of nineteenth-century homes, businesses, and articles of daily life, presented in a highly enjoyable, authentic manner. Throughout the state one finds historical homes and museums that may be toured for two or three dollars each. Here, for the same price, one tours an entire community of more than forty original buildings, each faithfully decorated.

The longer you spend in this time capsule, the more you'll see, but plan on a minimum of an hour for a cursory exploration.

The inspirational Dyer Memorial Chapel begins the self-guided tour. Reverend Dyer never had his own chapel, but crossed the mountains on foot between Oro and Breckenridge, summer and winter. One Sunday he walked eight miles from Buckskin Joe to Montgomery, intending to preach. But all the town, except for one man, was out staking claims on Quartzville. Dyer joined them and preached to thirty men.

The South Park Brewery houses the actual "museum" of South Park City. Its fine displays and historical background alone are worth the entrance price.

The romance of a bygone era is overwhelming at South Park City. The cleanly swept, wide, wooden sidewalks lead past the covered well, stage barn, homestead, narrow-gauge train, assay office, bank, and newspaper room. Where are the hopeful miners, the grubstakers, the Chinese workers, the hermit up the hill, and the blacksmith? They're all that's missing.

The men worked hard, there's no doubt, but so did the burros, whose long ears always seem to be in need of a gentle petting. With burro smiles on their faces, they worked side by side with the miners. Photos of them are housed in a former coal company office.

Rache's Place is the town's one saloon, which bustled with action when it was in the town of Alma. Its maroon walls echo the rich gleam of wood from the carved bar. The stuffed owl on the very top kept a keen eye on the gamblers who played during all-night sessions.

Also from Alma is the bank. Although it's not rich with marble columns, it presents an appropriately somber atmosphere with its dark walls and iron gratings.

Everywhere are unexpected sights. Outside the roost barn, with its few chicks, is a hand-held plow just like the one granddad used to turn the virgin South Dakota soil. The homestead is papered with *The Fairplay Flume* of 1879. (When cabins are dismantled, newspaper that was used as insulation often helps date the construction.) The four-foot-long marble soda fountain in Merriam's Drug Store is spectacularly ornate with its sixteen dispensers.

The mountains of the Mosquito Range peer over the Main Street buildings. Sheep, Peerless, Sheridan, Pennsylvania, and hollowed-out Horseshoe mountains all contained rich mineral deposits that led to the 1860s gold boom. They make a most appropriate backdrop to this visit to nineteenth-century Colorado mountain living.

Prunes Monument

5th and Front streets, Fairplay.

☐ Had he been human, Prunes would have had a retirement dinner followed by laudatory speeches and the presentation of a gold watch. But since he was a burro, his only reward for fifty years of faithful service to the miners was a decent burial, complete with a monument.

Beneath the bronze plaque on his memorial are his last four horseshoes and a worn leather halter, as well as a faded flyer that proclaims Fairplay the "Burro Capital of the World."

Burros played a vital role during the mining era by hauling in the provisions and hauling out the ore. Every July, Fairplay celebrates their contributions with the thirty-mile Burro Race up Mosquito Pass.

The Diggings

Just north of both Fairplay and Breckenridge.

☐ If only the Sierra Club had been around to tell the greedy miners a thing or two about environmental impact.

The first gold seekers of 1859 laboriously worked the streams with pans, placer mining for gold-bearing sand. Open-ended sluice boxes increased efficiency, but the sand and gravel had to be shoveled in by hand, and miners complained. Enter the Chinese in 1873. They may have complained just as loudly, but not too many understood them. The Fairplay Chinese community was forced to live "across the river," on the west side of the South Platte. Those with a good eye are still finding Chinese coins, opium bottles, and bits of porcelain.

Hydraulic machinery dramatically increased profits, but we're living with the side effects. Jet streams of water, focused against stream banks and bottoms, washed the sand and gravel through the sluice boxes as before, but in greater volume and with less labor. The result was greater profit and miles of sterile, unsightly gravel mounds.

Bristlecone Pine Scenic Area

Eight miles north of Fairplay on Hoosier Pass.

☐ Bristlecones are often the highest trees on a mountain before miniature tundra plants take over. Here on Mt. Bross's exposed Windy Ridge, they dare the alpine winds to bend their thick trunks to the ground. Tenaciously, their roots hold them tightly as they stretch sideways, as if sheltering themselves from the prevailing northern storms.

Windswept bristlecones live longer than anything else on earth. One Californian tree is thought to be 4500 years old, making the giant sequoias seem like youngsters.

BUENA VISTA

St. Elmo

☐ High above the Chalk Cliffs southwest of Buena Vista, St. Elmo's clapboard hotels, restaurants, and general stores stand vacant. More than thirty years have passed since customers were served in this 1880s gold camp, which is now one of Colorado's best preserved ghost towns.

By the early 1880s, the community of 2000 had three hotels, five restaurants, a drugstore, and a still-standing schoolhouse. The area was rich with ore, especially the Mary Murphy Mine just a mile south of town, which produced more than $60 million worth of gold and employed hundreds.

By 1930, only 300 townsfolk remained. The last to leave was the Stark family, headed by Anna Stark, who ran the Hotel Comfort for more than fifty years.

On the way to St. Elmo's along Highway 162 is a nineteenth-century hot springs swimming pool. The Chalk Cliffs on the right side of the road may still hold the cache of gold that legend says was hidden three hundred years ago by conquistadores fleeing from Indians. The old townsite of Alpine was home to only 500, but it had the big-city amenities of its own newspaper, a stage stop, two hotels, and three banks.

The road from Alpine to St. Elmo runs along the old narrow-gauge right-of-way of the Denver, South Park, and Pacific to St. Elmo.

This same company completed the mammoth Alpine Tunnel, which bored under 1800 feet of the Continental Divide southwest of town. More than 450 men worked at $3.50 a day for more than two years to complete the tunnel, which operated only until 1910.

Cottonwood Pass

West of Buena Vista.

☐ How about a picnic on the highest road pass in the United States? You may spend more time with a camera or binoculars than with the peanut butter sandwich, but who's complaining?

Driving on U.S. 285 from Antero, the summits of the Collegiate peaks rise into view one at a time. First it's Shavano, Tabequache, and Antero, then Princeton, Yale, Columbia, and Harvard. Chaffee County has twelve fourteeners, more than any other county in Colorado; with ten of them visible from the highway, they form the most formidable mountain barrier in the state.

An eighteen-mile drive west from Buena Vista leads to Cottonwood Pass, one of the highest mountain regions in the Rockies. The view from the 12,126-foot-high grassy ridge is to the wilderness side of the Collegiate Range: Harvard and Columbia mountains loom over the upper Texas Creek Basin. Except for this road, the area can be reached and seen only after miles of high-country hiking.

This might be a day to dine early, as thunderstorm buildups often begin around noon. Throw the gloves, caps, and jackets in the back seat and tell the maitre d' to save a rock with a view.

Stampede to Timberline:
The Ghost Towns and
Mining Camps of Colorado

by Muriel Sibell Wolle

Wolle, an art professor, sketched, poked around, studied, and interviewed people about the Colorado Rockies for a decade before writing this account of 240 mining camps. Never a dry historian but always an artist, Wolle records the heroic pioneer effort of the thousands of men who swarmed to the mountains, scrambled over its rocks, and panned its gullies.

CHAPTER 5

DENVER-PLUS

DENVER
LITTLETON
ENGLEWOOD
ARVADA
WHEAT RIDGE
GOLDEN
MORRISON
EVERGREEN
BOULDER

DENVER

Four Mile Historic Park _____

715 S. Forest St., Denver. Closed Mondays. Tours begin on the hour, 11–5. 399-1859.

☐ Once pioneers halted their wagons at Four Mile House, the ordeal was nearly over. They'd traveled hundreds of desolate miles through the wilderness of Kansas Territory and now were but four miles from the intersection of Broadway and Colfax, within hollering distance of the boom gold-rush camps of Denver and Auraria.

Oxen teams would be put to pasture along with any livestock that had been driven along the trail. Four Mile House had the last good grazing before reaching Denver, and the large corral meant there'd be no need to round up cattle the next day. Camps were formed next to Cherry Creek and within sight of the fabled Rockies.

The jostled, dusty passengers who arrived by stage wouldn't spend the night. They'd freshen up, and perhaps slip into the tavern while waiting for a new team to be harnessed for the ride to Denver. Fresh horses made a good impression on bystanders, helping to drum up business for the return trip.

Beginning in 1860, Four Mile House (built illegally on Indian land) served as a wayside inn and tavern used by soldiers, mountain men, prospectors, and farmers. The Butterfield Overland Dispatch made stops regularly, and business was good.

But when the railroad arrived in 1870, stage traffic dried up. Fortunately, the owners of Four Mile House had accumulated more than 600 acres and, with a successful irrigation system

based on water from Cherry Creek, the farm
prospered for nearly a century.

If you arrive at Four Mile House by foot or
bike along the Cherry Creek jogging trail from
either Monaco or Colorado boulevards, you'll
most closely simulate the early pioneer experience, since pioneers always followed the water
when possible and never drove cars.

Actually, the very best way to come is not
only along the trail but with grandparents.
They'll find dozens of reminders of their child-
hoods and their reminiscing will add to everyone's understanding and pleasure.

The former stage house is one of the many
buildings in Four Mile Historic Park, a twelve-
acre living history museum that retraces the
historical development of the Cherry Creek
Valley. The Park reflects the prairie, a stock
ranch, a stage stop, a dry-land farm, and an
irrigated farm.

Volunteers give tours of Four Mile House
throughout the day. It is a roughly built cabin
attached to a substantial brick home that was
added in the 1870s. The two-story cabin dates
from 1859, making it Denver's oldest existing
home. An early owner was a hardy pioneer who
ran the inn along with her two teenagers. She
slept on a lower bed, while they slept toe-to-toe
above her in a narrow but extra-long bed. A
trunk and washstand were the only other
furniture.

A large garden is carefully tended by volunteers, who till and irrigate crops in a well-
documented, nineteenth-century manner. Many
volunteers wear long skirts and calico bonnets,
or heavy work pants fastened with large buttons
and held up by suspenders.

Often Buck and Bright will be in the fields as
well. This young oxen team has been trained

to do the heavy work, although with only two
ploughed acres, life is a breeze for them.

Colorado Capitol _____

*1475 Sherman St., Denver. Summer tour hours are
every half hour, Monday-Friday, 9–3:30. Winter, call
ahead. 866-2604.*

☐ A visit to the capitol is one of the better free
tours in the state. Outside, it's beautifully pro-
portioned, a smaller version of the nation's
capitol. City-wide views of the gold dome are so
enjoyed that building permits are not granted to
skyscrapers that would block vision of the dome
from selected vantage points.

The dome was originally covered with 200
ounces of twenty-four-karat gold; another 43
ounces were added in 1980.

Walking up to the main entrance, the visitor
notices one step marked as exactly one mile
high. The notice was a good PR idea, but the
surveyor must have been a little short of oxygen
that day—his measurement is three steps short
of a mile.

Inside, details from doorknobs to marble
floor-insets proudly reflect Colorado's heritage.
Even bronze-paneled elevator doors depict state
history.

The Colorado History Museum _____

*1300 Broadway, Denver. Tuesday-Saturday, 10–4:30;
Sunday, 12–4:30.*

☐ The newly completed, sophisticated displays
of the State Museum are housed in the Heritage
Center, which is also the administrative home
of the Historical Society. The names are a little
complicated, but once inside the sleek interior,
there's a lot to be learned.

A time line extends the length of the lower floor; many photos and objects help the dates come alive. Showcases feature early Denver, the Plains Indians, and Mesa Verde. A replica of a sod house and Denver's first log cabin add immediacy to the displays.

Many of the best parts of the museum are reserved for schoolchildren who supplement their study of Colorado history with society programs. Thousands have spent a day in the Broadway School, a one-room schoolhouse with blackboards, prim aphorisms, and dark furnishings. Saturday morning programs, which require pre-registration, put children to work grinding corn, learning to lasso, setting up a tepee, or singing a cowboy ballad.

Forney Transportation Museum ⸻

1416 Platte St., Valley Hwy. and Speer Blvd., Denver. Monday-Saturday 9–5, Sunday 11–5. 433-3643.

☐ Big Boy is the star of the show. All 1,189,500 pounds of him sit outside in the crowded train yard. After clocking one million miles, he was retired in 1962 and donated to the Forney by the Union Pacific Railroad.

Big Boy is one of the largest steam locomotives in the world. Twenty-five similar models were built in the 1940s and only seven remain.

The Forney chronicles America's transportation history from wooden bicycles to Model-T pie wagons.

Denver Children's Museum _____

2121 Crescent Dr., 23rd Ave. exit from I-25. 10–5
Tuesday-Saturday; Fridays 'till 9 P.M. 12–5 Sunday.
Closed Mondays. 433-7444.

☐ Be prepared once you pass through the doors
and pay admission. The many changing exhibits
encourage youngsters from ages three to eleven
to explore motion, environment, energy, and
vision through hands-on learning.

The idea behind it all is to provide a majestic
vision for children in which imagination reigns.
Within the walls, some of which are even trans-
parent so the pipes and wiring are visible, are
exhibits that blend imagination, fact, and fun.

The best things never change. One is the
Ball Room, where children dive and scuffle
through eighty thousand plastic balls. Another
standard is the Circus Tent, where children
transform themselves with face painting.

Denver's museum is one of a handful nation-
wide that were built from scratch specifically
for children. Filling twenty-four thousand square
feet with innovative experiences is a challenge,
and so far, most children are pleased with the
results.

Denver Museum of Natural History _____

City Park, at intersection of Colorado and Montview
blvds. Daily, 9–5. 370-6363 for information on tours
and free days.

☐ What began as a small collection housed in a
drafty log cabin has become the nation's seventh-
largest natural history museum.

For many, the first-floor diplodocus and
stegosaurus that tower far above curious eyes
are reason enough to stop regularly at the

museum. These fellows were disinterred from
Garden Park, Colorado, where they roamed,
trampled forests, and munched on everything
green in sight.

The upstairs dioramas are also justly famous.
Each thriving blade of grass and leaf has been
handmade – many of us refuse to believe they're
not really alive. Dioramas of American Indian
life represent tribes from the Everglades to the
Arctic. Seventy-five animal habitat groups give
close-up encounters with the wild and wooly
creatures, including the pristine polar bear with
his haunting stance.

The collections seem endless. Birds with
their eggs are arranged from the tiniest to the
gigantic. The mineral section features Colorado
rocks, including a 114-pound volcanic stone that
contains the most gold ever preserved in a
single Colorado specimen.

There's obviously too much here for even the
most fanatic museum devotee. TIP: Choose a
favorite area, look at it all, and then enlarge
your sights with later visits.

The museum is in the same complex as the
Planetarium and the IMAX Theater. For those
who catch museum-mania, combination tickets
allow entrance to the museum as well as to the
theater or planetarium.

Outside the museum is the much-loved bronze
statue, *The Grizzly's Last Stand.* Follow his gaze
across City Park to a lake where paddleboats
are a sure cure for museum-worn feet.

IMAX

Lawrence Phipps IMAX Theater in the Denver Museum of Natural History at City Park, Colorado and Montview blvds. Combination tickets are available that include museum entrance. Information: 370-6300.

☐ They call it the cinema of the future, but how will a four-and-a-half-story-tall screen fit into a shopping mall cinema?

Images explode on the three-thousand-square-foot IMAX screen. The popular film *Hail Columbia!* shows a rocket on the screen that is just a little smaller than the actual rocket. At lift-off, the sound of the igniting engines is so penetrating that even clothing vibrates.

A six-channel system with thirty speakers generates sounds including frequencies lower than those which can be heard by the human ear. So the audience, sees, hears, and feels the image.

This is the only IMAX Theater within a thousand-mile radius and the only acoustically designed IMAX Theater in the world. The best seats are as close to the middle as possible; no late seating is permitted.

Gates Planetarium

Inside main entrance to the Denver Museum of Natural History at City Park, Colorado and Montview blvds. Recorded schedule: 370-6351. Astronomy phone for current astronomical information: 370-6316.

☐ Cities and stargazing just aren't compatible. Distant airplanes always look like satellites; stars under one magnitude are no competition for megawatt street lights; and nighttime idlers gazing upward generate neighborhood curiosity.

Gates Planetarium more than solves the problem. Newly remodeled, its facilities are among the best in the world. A compact star machine duplicates the magic of the night. Varied programs include "ZAP," a descriptive spectacle of lightning; and "Whirlpools of Darkness."

Gates Planetarium Laser Light Shows

Denver Museum of Natural History. Shows nightly, Wednesday-Sunday; and weekend afternoons. Call 370-6487 for recording.

☐ The staid planetarium, where just minutes earlier the mysteries of exploring galaxies were being analyzed, transforms itself when the incessant beat of rock vibrates from its black walls. This is the only laser show in a several-state area.

Regardless of what program is showing, the first Sunday evening of every month (7 P.M.) is dedicated to "Colorado Skies." Viewers get an in-depth preview of the stars, planets, and constellations and other celestial events visible in the coming month.

The Denver Mint

320 W. Colfax Ave. Twenty-minute tours weekdays leave every 30 minutes. 8:30–3; Wednesday, 9–3. 844-3582.

☐ The Denver Mint is one of the biggest tourist attractions in Denver. All summer, patient visitors line up under an awning, waiting for the next tour to begin.

With armed guards undoubtedly watching for false moves, everyone follows tour directions carefully. No one would think of turning left when the guide says "right."

The first view of the production line is from a government-green room lined with windows. Below, thousands of pennies and nickels seem

to be pouring from machines, making a substantial din. The tour guides appropriately stop
guiding, and everyone just looks.

The next stopping point is even louder, as
coins are being stamped. You call it: Which is
stamped first, heads or tails? Sorry. Both sides
are imprinted at once.

No wonder there's so much racket. More
than twenty million pennies are turned out daily,
plus all the nickels, dimes, and quarters. It's a
big, serious operation.

At the end of the tour are 402 ounces of pure
gold in bars, but these are just a fraction of
what's stored safely away from public view.
The Denver Mint is the largest U.S. gold
depository outside of Ft. Knox.

The short tour leaves no time for the mint's
history. An early branch mint at Sixteenth and
Market streets was the town's most substantial
building in 1863. Women and children used it as
a refuge from anticipated Indian raids.

A gift shop sells coin sets, medals, and
freshly stamped money: pay a dollar to push a
button, and a 90 percent copper coin is stamped,
just for you.

Molly Brown House _____

1340 Pennsylvania St., Denver. Closed Mondays.
832-1421.

☐ As with almost all home tours, the focus is
on the house—its curtains, carpets, and
curios—far more than on the personalities of the
occupants. What a loss. After all, people and
their unique stories are the stuff of life.

Molly was one of Denver's characters. She
married J.J. Brown in Leadville, and his one-
eighth interest in the Little Johnny Mine eventually brought them wealth. They moved to

Denver, settled on Pennsylvania Street, and Molly began her attempts to enter Denver society. It was not until her heroic survival of the Titanic disaster that she was accepted by the leading matrons of Denver.

The home is interesting as a period piece, but as the costumed guides point out, few pieces are original to the Browns.

Pearce-McAllister Cottage

1880 Gaylord St., Denver. Wednesday-Saturday, 10–4; Sunday, 12–4. 866-3508.

☐ The Colorado Historical Society does a good job wherever it goes. This 1899 middle-class home is one of its latest projects. This home is noteworthy because so many of its furnishings are original. The museum now houses the Denver Museum of Miniatures, Dolls, and Toys.

Denver Firefighters Museum

1326 Tremont Pl. (one block from the U.S. Mint), Denver. Weekdays, 11–2. 892-1436.

☐ Date: 1919
Place: Denver Fire House No. 1.
Time: 2:10 A.M.

The fire alarm sounds.

Men pull on their boots and slide rapidly down one of six poles from the second floor dormitory.

Meanwhile, the eleven on-duty horses move automatically from their stalls to suspended harnesses. Wagons are hitched and the team is galloping to the rescue within seventeen seconds of the first alarm.

And that's the way it was in Denver from the

1880s until the first motorized engine arrived in 1923.

Denver's numerous early fires were fought with a volunteer force wearing leather helmets. After the big fire of 1866, serious equipment was purchased. The museum displays a rare pumper from 1867; incredibly, oxen pulled it across the plains from Cincinnati!

More than 200 photos line the walls, giving a fascinating record of Denver's early years. With the guide's insight, they become living history. What about the fire chief who slept in an apartment in the back of the fire station? Or the photo of ten men holding a life net below a flaming building? The guide knows about them all.

Children make their own fun here. Those older than two-and-a-half years can stand in a fire truck and disappear under a red fire hat. For many, this is their first close-up look at firemen's equipment. It's a very positive introduction.

Upstairs is the spartan dormitory, as well as the fire records that hold much of Denver's history. The report for July 27, 1909, partially reads: "Between 16th and 17th on Stout Street wagon hit a buggie. Don't know what or who the owner is. Did not stop to inquire."

After touring, you'll be as hungry as a hard-working fireman. What luck, then, that the museum has a small restaurant upstairs – the Old Number One – serving homemade soups and sandwiches.

Black American West Museum

608 26th Street at Welton, Denver. Wednesday-Friday, 10–2; Saturday, 10–5; Sunday 2–5. 295-1026.

☐ Few people realize the role that blacks played in the taming of the West. But nine blocks east

of downtown Denver is a museum housing the
world's largest collection of Black American
Western history. The 5000 artifacts, tapes, and
photos on display are the result of twenty-two
years of relentless collecting and interviewing
by Paul Stewart, the museum's founder and
curator.

The photographs – grouped into mining, home-
steading, ranching and cowboys, and business –
speak most eloquently: a group of blacks head
west in a Mormon wagon train; a bonneted
pioneer leans stoically against the doorframe of
her sod house; the spirited workers of the Free
Men Mining Company pose next to a juniper tree.

The museum successfully conveys the magnitude of the proud, heart-wrenching drama
played out on the harsh frontier. Searching for
freedom and independence, blacks streamed
west by the thousands, working as cowpokes
and carpenters, musicians and miners, founding
their own towns, newspapers, businesses, and
even their own cavalry.

Every gallery holds surprises. Buffalo Soldiers
– so named because their thick dark hair
reminded the Indians of buffalo fur – document
the black contribution to the army as mappers,
interpreters, and guides for the fur traders of
the 1700s. Decades later, blacks were among
the throngs of prospectors headed deep into the
Rockies in search of gold. Forty blacks lived in
the Colorado mining town of Idaho Springs before
1900. A photo of a Mr. Bradley, for example,
shows him by the entrance to his Bertoli Saloon,
purchased with the earnings from a strike.

Denver Zoo

North side of City Park. Daily, 10–5. 331-4110.

☐ Zoo animals always look well fed. So it may come as a surprise that felines fast every Monday. It's not their punishment for sleeping through the visitor hours on the previous Sunday but an attempt to simulate a natural environment.

Feeding times for them are right on the button at 3:30 for the rest of the week. Lions spend much of their day snoozing, just as in the wild, where they often sleep up to twenty hours a day.

Other animals eat in the afternoons as well: sea lions at 2:30, monkeys at 3:00, and those hungry penguins at 10:15 and 4:00.

The Zoo is one of Denver's most popular attractions, with more than one million visitors yearly. Surprisingly, it's almost as busy in winter as in summer. Except for the exotic birds like the crested screamer, the pelican, and the stork, animals can expect little special winter treatment. Monkeys are kept inside instead of on their island; the outdoor animals manage on their own.

"Bird World" and elephants have long been the most popular attractions. Elephants spend almost as much time eating as lions do sleeping. In fact, their teeth literally wear out with all the munching, so they grow several sets during a lifetime, including new eight-pound molars.

Some of the more rare animals include the little Przewalski horses, which are among fewer than four hundred Mongolian wild horses in existence. The red panda, near the camels, is a nocturnal relative of the giant panda.

An animal nursery is part of the animal hospital. Orphaned babies and others requiring special care are on view to the public.

Buffalo Herds _____

Genesee Park. Adjacent to I-70, west of Denver twenty miles. Daniel's Park. Daniel's Park Rd., south off County Line Rd., twenty miles south of Denver.

☐ For the few dozen bison in the Denver Mountain Parks' herds, life has never been easier. No prairie fires to outrun. No arrowheads to dodge. No rifles to escape. No need to roam hundreds of miles for good prairie grasses.

Who knows how many buffalo were in a thirty-mile-long herd. The guess is that the hoof-prints of some seventy million once covered North America. White men's delight in killing for sport and profit was astounding, however, and within fifty years fewer than 1000 remained, according to naturalist Ernest Thompson. Thanks to legislation and rancher Charles Goodnight's efforts, the bison were saved and now number about 30,000.

Denver's largest herd is in Daniel's Park, but the I-70 herd is conveniently near the highway and almost always within camera range.

Denver Botanic Gardens_____

1005 York St., Denver. Daily, 9–4:45. 331-4010.

☐ What animals could hide behind that gigantic leaf?

Is a peony really "pleasingly plump?"

Which flowers do bumble bees like best?

Granted, learned horticulturists might cringe, but these are the questions that bring sparkle to every family's tour.

Denver Botanic Gardens are ripe for all kinds of discovery games. The twenty outdoor acres are densely planted to illustrate magnificent diversity. Wide, intricate pathways are for exuberant children to explore. Frequent benches and tranquil ponds are for their more contemplative, exhausted parents. The gardens accommodate everyone.

The intimate grounds of Shofu-en encompass handcrafted bridges, stone lanterns, and a tea house. Life is so tranquil here than sunbathing turtles rest for hours, not paying any attention to busy dragonflies, goldfish, or butterflies.

It takes a hands-and-knees approach to really enjoy the herb garden. Just touch your hands to the lemon balm and see how good it smells.

The vegetable section is a chance to experience lettuce and carrots before they reach their cellophane wrappers. Some cabbage varieties are bigger than mid-sized toddlers.

In most museums, children see displays from the bottom up. Throughout the gardens but particularly in the Alpine Garden with its multi-levels, children can experience the plants at eye level.

There's no way to see and enjoy the gardens in one visit. My favorite time to visit the soaring, indoor conservatory is during the chill of winter, when Denver is dreary and drab. Hibiscus bloom as if to spite the snow, and mangos and papayas bear fruit as bountifully as their Central American counterparts. The majestic royal palm, unaware of its protected state, has grown tall, as if threatening to break the protective glass roof and experience Colorado on its own.

Just breathing the luxuriantly moist air is a pleasure, enhanced by trickling streams and waterfalls. At least five types of fruit trees bloom and produce, but they're nothing in comparison to the exotic Lipstick Plant, Traveller's Tree, Elephant's Ear, and Earth Stars. Who was in charge of names, anyway?

The common supermarket varieties are here as well: baby tears, impatiens, dumb cane, and philodendron. The avocado flourishes, making it hard to believe this one started life in a glass on the windowsill, suspended by three toothpicks. No picnics allowed in the gardens, but across the street is Congress Park, with acres of grass and a swimming pool.

Platte River Greenway System _____

☐ Denver has the largest city park system in America. So is it a surprise that a few blocks from downtown is the nation's only white-water kayak course that runs within city limits?

Kayaks, rafts, and inner tubes are the only vessels now cruising the Platte, but misled entrepreneurs once launched a steamboat they hoped would carry fares to Brighton. Predictably, the boat was grounded within blocks. But these 1887 entrepreneurs were undaunted. They dammed the Platte at Nineteenth Street, backing up deeper water to Fifteenth Street. Paying passengers traveling its limited route were entertained by an opera company singing Gilbert & Sullivan.

People aren't the only ones appreciative of the Platte redevelopment project that began in 1974. Life of all kinds is returning to the river.

Colorado Greenway Demonstration Trail

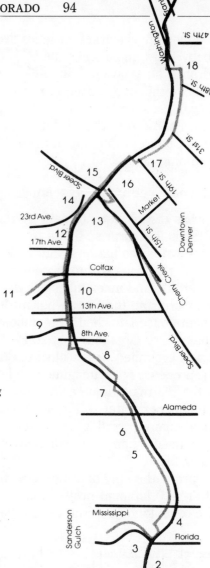

*Platte River
Greenway Trail*

1. Frontier Park
2. Pasquinel's Landing
3. Ruby Hill Park
4. Overland Pond
5. Vanderbilt Park
6. Habitat Park
7. Valverde Park
8. Frog Hollow
9. Weir Gulch Marina
10. Zuni Whitewater
    Chute
11. Lakewood Gulch/
    Rude Park
12. Gates-Crescent
    Park
13. Centennial Park
14. Fishback Landing
15. Confluence Park
16. Cherry Creek Park
17. Riverfront Park
18. Globeville Landing

Miles

 N

An early morning stroll may produce sightings of beavers, ducks, geese, muskrats, and blue heron.

The trail bordering the Denver portion of the river is 11.4 miles; the Colorado Greenway Demonstration Trail west to Kipling adds a seventeen-mile loop. Along the way are hundreds of acres of grassy and natural open spaces, with many "pocket" parks.

The biggest of these parks is Confluence, where Cherry Creek flows into the Platte. This is one of the most famous landmarks in the western states. It was a popular gathering spot for Plains Indians, and later for gold prospectors. At its Southeast corner, members of the Russell party founded Auraria in 1858. It was these fellows who started much of Colorado's gold rush.

The river is navigable from Frog Hollow (8) to Fiftieth Avenue (18), with the kayak course set up at Confluence Park (15). No water sports are encouraged when the river is running high. When the river calms and runs shallower, Arkansas River Tours conducts one-and-a-half hour rafting trips.

Elitch Gardens_____

W. 38th Ave. at Tennyson St., Denver. Summer. Sunday-Thursday, 10 A.M.–10 P.M.; Friday and Saturday 10 A.M.–11 P.M. Shortened hours in April, May, and September. 455-4771.

☐ Denver's Victorian-flavored amusement park may have a charming outdoor beer garden and flower-lined paths with quaint picket fences, but the rides give twentieth-century thrills.

The Twister has been rated number three in the nation on Cartmell's list of the ten most exciting roller coasters in North America. With a three-quarter-mile-long track, and speeds that reach sixty-three m.p.h., no one would dispute that rating, particularly those who sit in the last of the train's sixteen cars.

When the park opened in 1890 as a zoological garden in an old apple orchard, it was five miles outside of town, and visitors arrived by buggy, bicycle, and steam train. The Gardens have undergone many changes since founder Mary Elitch paraded the grounds in a peacock-drawn carriage. But from its earliest days, flowers have complemented the entertainment.

Some 25,000 square feet of greenhouse space are planted each year with seeds and cuttings and moved outdoors to the gardens in June. A hallmark has long been the hanging baskets, over 300 of which beautify walkways, arches, and corners of buildings.

In 1981 Elitch Theatre opened and over the years hosted a roster of legends including Sarah Bernhardt, Cecil B. DeMille, Douglas Fairbanks, and Talulluh Bankhead. More recent alumni are Mickey Rooney, Van Johnson, Lynn Redgrave, and Debbie Reynolds.

The saying still holds true: "Not to see Elitch's is not to see Denver."

Lakeside Amusement Park _____

4601 Sheridan Blvd., Denver. Summer. 477-1621.

☐ The spectacular roller coaster by the shores of Lake Rhoda has been keeping Denver screaming for years. There's no letting up in its twisting turns and breakneck descents. No wonder it's famous.

Lakeside has been entertaining Denver since 1908. In the park's early years, the lake was filled with swimmers, but eventually an indoor pool became the vogue.

One of the most popular rides has always been the miniature train ride around the lake. The train is powered by a 1903 steam engine. Small children enjoy their own small thrills in a well-equipped Kiddie Playland.

Denver Art Museum

100 W. 14th Ave. Pkwy. Within walking distance of the Denver Mint, the Capitol, and the State Museum. Sunday, 12–5; Tuesday-Saturday, 10–5; Wednesday until 8 P.M. 575-2793.

☐ People have fun here, and perhaps that's why it's one of the most frequently visited art museums in the country. The pleasure begins outside with the building's handsome, over-grown, tiled-fortress look.

American Indian and Eskimo works from several hundred tribes make up the largest collection. Clothing, beads, sculpture, carving, sand painting. . .they did it all, and did it all well.

The American art section on the third floor houses enormous paintings of trappers, mountains, and wild beasts, many painted by artists who'd never been west of the Mississippi. But then, that's no different from creating a sci-fi movie and never leaving Hollywood.

On the third and fourth floors are period rooms that let visitors experience original furnishings of different eras. The Mexican Tarascan house contains treasures from ancient Latin America, while the Duran Chapel is filled with carved santos of the Southwest. There are also period rooms from eighteenth-century America, as well as ones representing English Tudor, Spanish Baroque, and French Gothic styles.

The restaurant is a welcome addition for quick lunches.

The Museum of Western Art_____

1727 Tremont Pl. (in the Navarre Building, across the street from the Brown Palace), Denver. Tuesday-Saturday, 10–4:30. 296-1880.

☐ New museums are few and far between, but this addition to Denver's cultural life is a gem.

This comprehensive private collection gives Denver a fine overview of Western art. Yet the three-story collection is small enough to be thoroughly enjoyed without the exhaustion that usually accompanies museum outings.

Here is not only art but history. The paintings depict the West with its Indians, frontiersmen, settlers, and cowboys. The impact of expansionism is a theme of many later paintings.

The paintings that the *Christian Science Monitor* has called "perhaps the last great Western Art collection" hang in the Old Navarre, itself a cross-section of the West. Built in 1880, this landmark opened as a school for young girls, but within the decade it briefly became a hotel with a lower floor gambling casino. At the turn of the century, it became a restaurant, serving Denver's society for nearly seventy-five years. The present owner renovated the property, reopening it as a museum in 1983.

Larimer Square_____

1400 block of Larimer Street, lower downtown Denver. 534-2367 for information on special events.

☐ When General William E. Larimer hit town in 1858, Denver City wasn't much to behold. In fact during its first year, only one block of stores was to be found. Huddled on the banks of Cherry Creek, they became the nucleus of the supply town growing up on the plains, and five years later, 150 homes clustered around what is now Larimer Square.

The original rough structures are long burnt down, replaced with sturdy brick buildings representing Denver's increasing importance. Eighteen of these Victorian structures remain and have become the centerpiece of Denver's lower downtown preservation efforts.

Street parties routinely close the block to traffic, as the Square is the site of many of the city's festivals, as well as being an excellent choice for a stroll, with plenty of shops and restaurants along the way.

Denver Center for the Performing Arts

1245 Champa St., Denver. Free guided tours during the summer at noon from the theater box office. During the season, call for appointment. 893-4000.

□ It's sleek. Sophisticated. Stimulating. And fun!

The soaring glass archway is straight from the twenty-first century, as is the slender sculpture *Infinite Energy,* which directs eyes upward. Below the elaborate glass roof is generous space for gazing, gathering, and enjoying the nation's most complete performing arts center.

A forty-five minute noon tour takes you to the three theaters of the Helen Bonfils Theatre Complex. You'll have a chance to peek backstage into the dressing rooms of the stars, sit in the sumptuous pastel seats, and exclaim over the innovative decor of Boettcher Concert Hall with its 109 suspended acrylic discs.

The Shops at Tabor Center

16th Street Mall at Lawrence Street, Denver.

☐ No mere shopping center this. It's two blocks of glass and a galleria that brings the outdoors in, no matter what the weather. Locals love it, but so do visitors. Over 900,000 out-of-towners ride its escalators and admire its pastel banners every year. But how many notice that the main fountain, which spurts in a seemingly inconsistent pattern, is computerized to follow the movements of the glass elevator?

At the east end of Tabor Center is the D&F Tower, one of Denver's most famous landmarks. It's all that's left of what was an exclusive fashion store.

Tabor Center, a Rouse development, stands on the site of the 1879 Tabor Block and follows the same tradition of innovation. Built by the mining millionaire Horace Tabor, it was Denver's first building over four stories tall and boasted the city's first elevator, first national bank, and stashed in the attic, Denver's first telephone company.

Cranmer Park

3rd Ave. and Cherry St., Denver.

☐ An oversized Chinese sundial takes center stage. The thick shadow it casts tells accurate time to within minutes.

A large native flagstone promenade gives an elegant air to this observation point. Along its perimeter is inlaid information on many of the famous mountains visible from Cranmer Park.

The Pikes Peak inscription tells how Zebulon Pike began the first attempt on his namesake by walking from Pueblo. Three days later he stood waist high in snow, with no blankets, food, or socks. He turned back, muttering something about unpredictable Colorado weather.

The Museum of Outdoor Arts_____

The Greenwood Plaza office complexes radiate from E. Orchard Road and S. Syracuse Way, Englewood.

☐ Real estate developers talk a lot about environmental enhancement, but few do much about it. The John Madden Company is a notable exception. His projects – Marin III, Quebec Court, Harlequin Plaza, and Orchard Falls – successfully blend architecture, landscape, and the fine arts. The employees in these buildings are lucky, and so is the public, as we're invited for leisurely strolls, workdays or not, to enjoy the treasures.

Even the light fixtures on S. Syracuse Circle and E. Orchard Road have a story to tell: they're copies of ones cast by Michelangelo and can't be seen anywhere else in the United States. Henry Moore's great "heroic" bronze sculpture, *Large Spindle Piece*, is the most prominent piece to date in the museum. Altogether, there are nineteen pieces to admire.

The Museum of Outdoor Arts' outdoor amphitheatre is used for summer concerts.

LITTLETON

Littleton Historical Museum_____

6028 S. Gallup St., Littleton. Monday-Friday 8–5, Saturday 10–5, Sunday 1–5. 795-3850.

☐ Suburban Denver hasn't always meant neighborhoods with exotically named curving streets and acres of mall parking.

Way back when, much of Littleton, Lakewood, Broomfield, and Wheat Ridge was farmland. In fact, Molly Brown herself kept a summer home, far from city noises, at the intersection of today's Yale and Wadsworth.

Developers' bulldozers have done their job, but contented moos and grunts from an active farm still emanate from Littleton's Historical Museum. The living history farm represents farm life typical of Littleton from 1895 to 1905.

Many early farmers were disgruntled prospectors from the East. The fertile foothills soil attracted more farmers, and by 1866, 400,000 acres had been claimed and settled in Colorado.

Families are encouraged to walk through the farmhouse and outbuildings. Being so close to town, these farmers lived in style: settees upholstered with horsehair, kerosene chandeliers, and fancy parlor stoves.

Everything on this farm is shipshape: the water wagon parked near the windmill, the privy sitting discreetly behind the farmhouse, and the toolshed, where blacksmiths still repair machinery.

And there are buildings for each of the animals. Chickens roost in the hen house, pigs sleep in the hog shed, horses in the barn, and cows in hay-padded stalls.

City kids quickly establish friendships with cows and horses. But the hogs, which in real life are far more formidable than our friends Porky and Petunia, take some getting used to. I asked one five-year-old why pigs were raised. In a questioning tone he replied, "For milk?"

Children who attended the log schoolhouse, Colorado's oldest, would sit on benches around the perimeter of the room and work at long tables that formed a rectangle around the central box stove. They began their day with hymns and patriotic songs, undoubtedly snickered through the teacher's inspirational remarks, and then settled down to hours of recitation and memorization.

Thirteen-acre Kettring Lake completes the farm's idyllic setting. A footbridge leads to a picnic-perfect island. Scores of ducks paddle contentedly, wisely enjoying the treats of conscientious duck-feeders.

The entrance to the farm is through a small museum whose changing exhibits highlight the past, as well as photography, arts, and crafts.

ENGLEWOOD

Belleview Park

W. Belleview Ave. and Huron St., Englewood. Miniature Train and Petting Zoo are open Memorial Day–Labor Day. Closed Mondays.

☐ Belleview Park is proof positive that Small is Wonderful.

A miniature train thunders under a tunnel, screeches over a trestle, and toots around untamed prairie, giving the best little ride in the state.

A petting zoo gives close-up experiences with grunting pigs, mellow donkeys, waddling ducks, and half-pint horses. These animals are each treated as the special pets they are by eager teenage wardens. None is just another sheep in a flock, goat in a herd, or goose in a gaggle. They thrive in the shade of their very own cottonwood tree, relax in the clean gravel pens, and gaze contentedly at the quaint red and white barn, perhaps hoping silently that they can doze a few moments before the next eager-to-pet Brownie troop bursts through the gate.

The contradiction in the name Big Dry Creek doesn't make it less appealing. Grassy banks run right down to its trickling, cool water as it winds its way through the park. Crossing a bridge and heading east, park visitors encounter Space Playground, where a red, white, and blue airplane obliges every would-be child pilot who fantasizes in its cockpit, or hangs precipitously from its wings.

ARVADA

Arvada Center for the Arts and Humanities

6901 Wadsworth Blvd., Arvada. Daily. 431-3080.

□ Like a futuristic geometric puzzle, the Arvada Center spreads across seventeen acres of rolling Hackberry Hill. It's a spectacular Front Range setting with dry fields, cottonwoods, and wide vistas of the Rockies. Contemporary marble sculptures dot grassy acres kept trimmed by busy rabbits. Dozens of entry stairs double as outdoor amphitheater seating for summer events.

The center is home to a children's theater, A Company of Players. This participatory theater group provides one of the main focuses for children's theater in Colorado. They perform in a five-hundred-seat auditorium also used for the Youth Symphony.

The center's museum presents local history in changing exhibits. On permanent exhibit is the Haines Cabin; small as it is, it was home to a family of eight. The Haines family came to Colorado by covered wagon in the 1860s and established its land claim through squatter's rights.

A two-floor gallery features dramatic architectural angles and open spaces. Exhibits vary monthly from traditional watercolors to America's folk art, from quilts to western scenes.

WHEAT RIDGE

Wheat Ridge Museum and Sod House __

4610 Robb St., Wheat Ridge.

☐ Yet another insight into Colorado history comes through a visit to a typical soddy.

Soddies were home to thousands of homesteaders throughout the plains states. Very few original ones remain, as they only withstood fierce winters and winds for about a dozen years before needing to be rebuilt. But the 1886 Wheat Ridge Soddy has needed only one wall repaired, and that because of vandals.

They were dark, cramped, and utilitarian. But with twenty-inch earthen walls, they were cool in the summer and warm in the winter.

Their furnishings were similar to the ones in Wheat Ridge: a wooden bathtub, a rough table, and tree-bark chairs. It was just enough of a home in which to raise a family of three children, a hundred years ago.

GOLDEN

Colorado Railroad Museum _____

17155 W. 44th Ave. (Exit 64 off I-70), Golden. Daily, 9–5. Summer, 9–6. 279-4591.

☐ The glory of the railroad era is alive and well in the shadow of Table Mountain. Inside the replica of an 1880s-style brick station are two floors of railroad bits and pieces: photographs of the men, such as General Palmer, founder of

the Denver and Rio Grande, who made their
fortunes from trains; and photographs of the
men, such as Oriental laborers, who made their
livings from trains.

The yards are littered with dozens of silent
engines and stationary Pullmans. Climb aboard
and play engineer, or stretch out on a berth and
imagine the plains sweeping past.

Colorado's oldest locomotive, the D&RG
Engine No. 346, has been retired to a half mile
of track; on some weekends and holidays it
steams up and makes a trip to the end of its line
before coming to rest again beside its wooden
water tower.

Buffalo Bill Memorial Museum and Grave

*I-70 west of Denver to exit 256, then follow signs.
Tuesday-Sunday, 10–4. 526-0747.*

☐ No museum can contain the legend of this
superman. Wild West posters and fancy six-
shooters, priceless Indian clothes, weapons, and
photos begin to hint at the fame that William
Cody achieved. But the real story has more
drama, finery, action, and daring than the
polished museum conveys.

Cody shot his first Indian just shy of the age
of eleven, and by fourteen was the youngest
Pony Express rider. He should be in the
Guinness Book of Records, or perhaps he is, for
carrying mail through 322 miles of hostile
territory in twenty-one hours and forty minutes,
going through twenty horses along the way.

Buffalo Bill's Wild West and Congress of
Rough Riders of the World Show must have been
spectacular. He played it throughout North
America before giving a command performance
for Queen Victoria at Windsor Castle.

An original Wild West program lists 600
performers. Hundreds of horses, buffalo, elk,
deer, and wild Texas steers completed the cast,
which played to appreciative audiences that
often included royalty. A photograph shows the
$100,000 cherry-wood bar that Queen Victoria
commissioned and sent to Cody's hotel in Wyoming after the command performance.

Flashy accessories have always been important in the showman's bag of tricks, and Buffalo Bill's were no exception. During thirty years with the Wild West Show he cultivated an extraordinary wardrobe of buckskin costumes. Thousands of beads in floral and patriotic patterns cover one jacket, which has three-inch fringes dripping from its waist, collar, sleeves, and yoke. Just as showy are his three favorite saddles, elaborately tooled with his likeness and inset with sterling-silver buffalo medallions.

Beaded buckskin costumes remind visitors of the many Indians who acted in the Wild West extravaganza, a swift turn of events considering that as late as 1876 Buffalo Bill scouted for Fifth Cavalry campaigns against the Sioux. Sitting Bull joined the troupe in 1885. A poignant photo shows nine befeathered Indian chiefs visiting Buffalo Bill's grave.

Coors Brewery

I-70 or Highway 6 to 13th and Ford, Golden. Shuttle is available from Visitor's Center, June-August, Monday-Saturday. Free half-hour tours from 10–4. Shuttles from 8:30 to 4:30. 277-2337.

☐ Taking a tour is almost as much of a production as making the beer. There's driving to Golden, busing to the brewery, waiting for the guide, passing security, and listening to a twenty-five minute talk on the intricacies of hops and barley while looking at humongous vats. Finally comes the tasting room where every swallow goes down as good as you knew it would.

This is the world's largest single brewing facility, using 13,640-gallon copper kettles. Over 300,000 visitors tour annually. Of course, many of those are students from nearby colleges, who have been known to come back more than once.

Foothills Art Center

809 15th St., Golden. Monday-Saturday, 9–4; Sunday, 1–4. 279-3922.

☐ History intertwines with art at the nationally recognized Foothills Art Center.

Steeply roofed, with a squat belfry, the First Presbyterian Church of Golden was dedicated in 1872, four years before Colorado became a state. Its first minister was the colorful circuit rider, Rev. Sheldon Jackson.

Almost a century later, the church had outlived its usefulness as a worship center and was on a downhill slide toward demolition. But a reprieve came in 1968. Pictures have replaced pews and art classes have replaced the Ladies Aid in this year-round facility for arts exhibitions.

Next door, Foothills II is an exhibit area for arts and crafts, while up and down the block are galleries and lunch spots. Many books and crafts are within a child's price range, especially during the Holiday Art Market, which begins in October and runs through early December.

Golden Gate Canyon State Park

Hwy. 58 to Golden, north on Washington St. to Hwy. 93. Turn up Golden Gate Canyon Road and continue fifteen miles. 592-1502.

☐ With ten thousand acres and forty-five miles of trails, there's plenty of room to spread out. Alert hikers will be rewarded by frequent sightings of mule deer and by chattering from some of the 150 bird species that have been sighted.

Those in the know say Golden Gate has the most wildflowers of any Front Range setting. Picnic tables are in the midst of the flower carpet, yet separated one from another by tall grasses. A series of ten ponds and miles of trout-stocked streams encourage fishing.

At the park's entrance is a rustic nature center, where rangers can give tips on hikes, camping, and fishing. Summer weekend and holiday campfire talks cover wildlife, gold panning, geology, and the like.

MORRISON

Red Rocks Amphitheater

One mile from I-70 near Morrison, twelve miles west of Denver.

☐ When no thunderstorms are threatening, Denver's most pleasant cultural center is Red Rocks, an eight-thousand-seat outdoor amphitheater sandwiched between Ship Rock and Crimson Rock. These high, red sandstone outcroppings provide natural acoustics, and the seats in between provide a dramatic view of Denver lights, lights that seem to stretch to Kansas.

The stars in the foothill skies are incredibly bright but no brighter than the forty to fifty musical artists playing in each summer's concert series. Seats are now reserved, so it's no longer necessary to take the day off from work to picnic and hold your group's seats. But don't let that deter you—it's still a laid-back way to spend an afternoon.

In this 600-acre park, roaming and photography are obvious pastimes.

EVERGREEN

Mount Falcon Park

Colo. 74, east from Evergreen. Or Highway 285 west of Denver to the Indian Hills exit. Signs direct from there.

☐ Views of Denver from Red Rocks Amphitheater are breathtaking. They're even better from Mount Falcon Park, because now they include not only Red Rocks but Mount Evans.

The park is a gem among the thousands of acres held by Jefferson County Open Spaces. From its many trails, one gets 200-mile vistas of plains, lakes, and even Pikes Peak.

John Brisben Walker was a mover and shaker in turn-of-the-century Denver. His dreams were large, and Colorado's beauty nurtured them. His four-thousand-acre estate included the park and Red Rocks. Once his own home was complete, Walker began a campaign to bring the summer White House to Mount Falcon; had he been successful, he would have been neighbor to the president.

Financing the "Presidential Retreat" proved impossible. One scheme included asking every American school child for a dime. But a 1926 electrical storm put an end to fundraising and dreams. Lightning struck and destroyed both his home and the foundations of the summer White House.

A tall fireplace and some foundations remain for visitors to wonder at. The view is as spectacular as it ever was.

Hiwan Homestead Museum

4208 Timbervale Dr., Evergreen. Forty-five-minute guided tours, Tuesday-Sunday. 674-6262.

☐ Some people never know when to stop. Imagine building additions onto a log cabin until it had seventeen rooms. You can see the result in the Hiwan Homestead Museum.

The home was begun in the 1880s by a woman who hired a local craftsman to build her dream home on 1280 acres of foothills land. As her dreams expanded, so did the house.

Many of the rooms re-create homestead life

in the 1880s, and other rooms are devoted to changing exhibits on Jefferson County history.

The museum is also noteworthy for its ambitious pioneer crafts programs for children. One room is always set aside for groups of children to practice crafts and domestic chores of the period.

BOULDER

Chautauqua Park

9th St. and Baseline Rd., Boulder, Parks and Recreation, 441-3408 for information on hikes.

□ It seems as if Colorado has always been a place for mountains.

Our Rocky Mountains have been with us for more than 50 million years. And before their time, a range existed that geologists call the Ancestral Rockies. This early formation was in place more than 300 million years ago. Erosion's slow but persistent hand did a job on these mountains and totally eliminated them. But the sediment that eroded gathered in horizontal layers, right where today's foothills are.

When our familiar Rockies were born, the foot-hills were turned on end and tilted dramatically. The spectacular red slabs seen along the eastern plains from Colorado Springs to Boulder are erosional remnants of the Ancestral Rockies. In Boulder, these "leftover" rocks are called the Flatirons.

The towering Flatirons rise dramatically from the southwestern boundary of Chautauqua Park, making it a trailhead for several good hikes. Self-guided McClintock Nature Trail begins behind the auditorium. The popular Mesa Trail ends six miles away in Eldorado Springs. The Royal Arch Trail starts at Bluebell Shelter

and continues two miles to the top of the Flatirons. The twenty-foot natural arch at the end of
the trail resulted from faulting and frost erosion.
The ranger cottage in the park is a good
source for information on trails. Rangers lead
half-day hikes Saturday mornings in the summer.
Chautauqua is also home to a large summer
festival of music, films, and lectures.

Boulder Public Library _____

9th St. and Canyon Blvd. 441-3100.

☐ Libraries and vacations aren't a usual juxta-
position. But the children's section here is so
well done that its concepts deserve to be seen
and imitated elsewhere.

The large children's library is housed in its
own section, reached by a covered walkway lined
with contemporary sofas overlooking the
greenery below. Books are within easy reach of
young readers. Youngsters read stretched out
on gigantic colored cushions or snuggled on
window seats overlooking the park. Young adults
have a separate music and reading room.

Although books provide the reason-to-be, the
library is a Mecca for all types of arts. There
are three art galleries, guest speakers, musical
performances, and free film programs.

Colorado Shakespeare Festival _____

*University of Colorado, Boulder. 492-2783 for
reservations.*

☐ Although forced marches through Julius
Caesar still keep English teachers occupied for
weeks on end, there is an alternative. You can
meet the bard under the stars.

The intimate Mary Rippon amphitheater is
home to the nation's most ambitious Shake-
spearean theater program. All thirty-seven of

Shakespeare's works have been presented since the outdoor program began in 1958.

Each summer three plays are featured in repertory during evening performances. Slabs of red Colorado sandstone provide seating for 1000. All of the seats are good, but without blankets, all become uncomfortable about ten minutes into act 2.

Outdoor theater provides its own rewards, though. In one performance of *A Midsummer Night's Dream,* a group of rabbits trooped across stage. During *Macbeth,* hail fell just as the witches were chanting, "All hail Macbeth."

The reputation and quality of the festival draws actors, directors, and designers from across the country. More than thirty performances are held each July and August.

Boulder Center for the Visual Arts

1750 13th St., Boulder. Tuesday-Saturday, 11–5; Sunday, 1–5. 443-2122.

☐ This gallery is absolutely non-intimidating. In fact, the comfortable former brick home, with its plank floors and high ceilings, is an ideal place to confront the stimulating work of local artists.

With eight openings a year, for two different shows displayed simultaneously, it's clear this is the anchor for Boulder art activities.

Boulder Historical Society Museum

1206 Euclid Ave., Boulder. Tuesday-Friday, 11:30–4; Saturday, 12–4. 449-3464.

☐ This small museum does its best to tell the story of Boulder and its dependency on water, ranching, and farming.

The lucky ones, as usual, are the kids. They can be part of the week-long summer sessions that concentrate on frontier life.

Eldorado Canyon State Park_____

Eldorado Springs, south of Boulder. 494-3943.

☐ Internationally famed for technical rock climbing, the park's sheer sandstone walls soar up to 850 feet above South Boulder Creek.

Climbing equipment isn't necessary, however, for picnicking, hiking, fishing, and enjoying the thousands of wildflowers in the 272-acre park. Some trails follow the creek; another takes off over Rattlesnake Gulch to ruins of a hotel.

Summer is hot in the canyon, but just minutes away in Eldorado Springs is an artesian-fed swimming pool with naturally heated waters. Grab a shower and jump in. The immediate surroundings are uninspiring, but look to the brilliant red of the Flatirons looming above.

Small People in Colorado Places

by Susan Kaye

This Front Range odyssey adventure takes families from the pinnacle of Pikes Peak to the cozy cabin of an 1860s homesteader. Its whimsical, refreshing style has made it a favorite of mothers, dads, teachers, and grandparents.

This extensive compilation of wonderful things includes a month-by-month calendar of children's fun and well answers the question "What shall we do now?"

CHAPTER 6

NORTHEAST

LOVELAND
FORT COLLINS
GREELEY
PLATTEVILLE
BURLINGTON

LOVELAND

The Sweetheart Town _____

☐ With such a romantic name, the city is a
ringer for Valentine promotions. Since 1947,
they've done it up right, stamping more than
4.5 million valentines with a special four-line
cachet and Cowboy Cupid.

To remember special friends, address and
stamp valentines as usual. Then place all
envelopes in an outer wrapper addressed to:

Postmaster
Attention: Valentines
Loveland, Colorado 80537

Send packages first class, making sure they
arrive no later than February 7. A Loveland
postmarked card is the next best thing to
sending Cupid in person.

Loveland Museum _____

*503 Lincoln Ave., Loveland. Weekdays, 9–5; Saturday,
10–4; Thursday until 9 P.M. 667-6070.*

☐ The Main Street exhibit of storefronts and a
hotel lobby well represents early Loveland.
The Wagon Shop is dominated by an enormous
bellows that feeds into the forge. It is said
that some smiths took better care of their fires
than of themselves.

The Dentist Shop looks formidable with its
foot-powered drill hanging ominously by the
patient's chair. The General Store is packed with
goods, including a wide selection of wire-rimmed
spectacles and bolts of fabric.

The Loveland Museum holds a large relief
of the Big Thompson Water Project. This
$162-million marvel gathers water on the western

side of the Continental Divide and transports it to the eastern side.

Big Thompson

□ Route 34 west from Loveland heads through the Big Thompson Canyon, through Estes Park, and over Trail Ridge Road. Altogether, it's one of the most scenic drives in the world.

The drama begins at the entrance to Big Thompson Canyon, four miles west of Loveland. For miles, two lanes snake beside the churning river, flanked by rock walls so high that sunlight reaches the valley floor only at midday. Red-barked ponderosa pines dot northern slopes; the southern exposure supports only bitter brush, mountain mahogany, and prickly pear cactus.

Here and there, the canyon widens to leave room for a handful of Indian curio shops, small lodges, and cider houses. Like a page from an old scrapbook, these are scenes from Colorado mountain living before the big resorts: mom-and-pop antique stores, log cabins, and the welcome comfort of a rocking chair on a shady porch.

Best stopping place is Viestenz-Smith Mountain Park, nine miles into the canyon. A well-kept grassy area of picnic tables and barbeques, it also records the July 1976 flood, the worst natural recorded disaster in Colorado. When ten to sixteen inches of rain fell in four hours, the river rose seventeen feet.

Two trails begin at the park. Round Mountain National Recreation Trail is a one-mile nature trail to a shelter overlooking the canyon. The other is a 4.75-mile one-way walk to the summit of Sheep Mountain.

The canyon ends as abruptly as it began, opening to a view over Estes Valley and Long's Peak.

FORT COLLINS

Fort Collins Museum _____

200 Mathews St., Fort Collins. Tuesday-Saturday,
10–5; Sunday, 12–5. 221-6738.

☐ The nicely done displays in the former library
change seasonally or, according to the man in
charge, "whenever we get tired of looking at
them."

The cowboys' section holds a cowboy hat
from the 1880s and various sinister-looking
tools, including a cow dehorning saw and a hog-
hide scraper. Farmers had their work cut out
for them with a beet-cutting knife, a hay knife,
and a cornstalk-cutting knife.

Three historic buildings sit in the shaded
Pioneer Courtyard in the back. The Janis Cabin
dates from the fur-trapping era and is one of
the oldest existing buildings in Colorado. Antoine
Janus filed papers for his homestead in 1844
when the Poudre Valley was "black with buffalo."

The Auntie Stone Cabin was Fort Collins's
first dwelling. Built in 1864, it was used as an
Officers' Mess while the fort was still active,
then as the first hotel and the first school.

GREELEY

The Meeker Home_____

1324 9th Ave., Greeley. Tuesday-Friday, 10–3 winter,
10–5 summer. 353-6123, Ext. 9221.

☐ When Horace Greeley of the New York *Tribune*
visited the area in 1859, he was impressed by
its agricultural potential. He eventually interested
Nathan Meeker, who organized the Union Colony
of Colorado with encouragement from Horace.
Union Colonists founded Greeley in 1870. Mem-

berships originally sold for fifteen dollars to
"men of strict temperance and good character."
    Greeley certainly forecast well: cattle and
fields of sugar beets, barley, corn, and other crops
remain the city's mainstay.
    Meeker's 1870 home has stood the test of time
as well. This forty-five-minute-plus tour gives
exhaustive information about the furnishings of
this dynamic man's home.

Centennial Village

*14th Ave. and A St., adjacent to Island Grove Park,
Greeley. Tours begin on the hour from April through
October, Friday 10–5 and weekends 1–5. 353-6123,
Ext. 9217.*

☐ Report to the train depot on arrival. Sit in
carved oak pews, make conversation with sightseers from around the country, and wait for the
energetic teenage guide to take you on a tour of
historic northern Colorado buildings from 1860
to 1920.
    The fifty-minute tours begin with a Cheyenne
tipi (identified by the thirteen tipi poles) and
end in a proper Victorian home. In between are
a homestead shack, a sod house, a rock house,
and a wagon house, vividly bringing to life
Colorado's homestead era. The claim shanty is
papered with newspapers. An interesting fact:
the Colorado plains provided so few trees that
settlers brought in cheap lumber for homes by
rail.
    Lone Valley School rivals the Broadway School
in Denver's State Museum for its old-time
appeal. The central stove was a standard feature,
as was the cyclone-cellar trap door by the
teacher's desk. Built in the early 1900s, the
school was attended by elementary children
near Akron.

The 1917 Zion Lutheran Church was used as a barn after its congregation built bigger quarters. Once it was moved to Centennial Village, volunteers dedicated thousands of hours to restore its beauty. The effort was successful. A pump organ sits near the altar and stained-glass windows soften the hot prairie sun.

Centennial Village is an ambitious centennial project and the small town of Greeley has carried it off well.

Centennial Trail

☐ James Michener celebrated northeastern Colorado in *Centennial,* which was centered around Greeley. Back in the late 1930s, Michener taught in Greeley's college. He explored the High Plains around the college town and thought about the challenges that faced the first settlers of the region. Nearly forty years later, he returned to the area and used it as the setting for his epic historical novel.

To follow the Centennial Trail, head east on U.S. 34 down the South Platte River Valley. The tree-lined river provided transportation to fur trappers, who were the first white men in the area. For a close look at the river much as

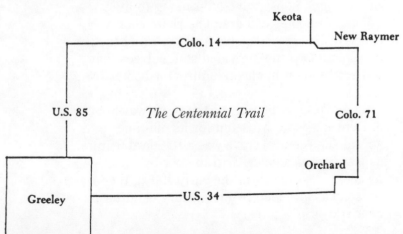

The Centennial Trail

it appeared in the mid-1800s, take a short detour north on Colo. 37 at Kersey. From where the highway crosses the river, the South Platte is seen as a placid, shallow stream, ideal for canoes.

Continuing east on U.S. 34, the trail passes the Monfort feedlots, the largest cattle-feeding operation in the world. A visitor center at the feedlots is open weekdays, providing an overview of the cattle industry.

About five miles east of Deerfield, the Centennial Trail takes a short detour north to Orchard on a country road. During the filming of "Centennial," Hollywood special effects teams changed Orchard into a frontier town, and remnants of their work can be seen on some main street buildings.

Outside of Fort Morgan, the trail heads north on Colo. 52 into the arid High Plains. The Centennial Trail turns west at the junction of Colo. 52 and Colo. 14 near New Raymer.

About seven miles west of New Raymer, the trail makes another detour north to Keota, once a thriving small community and now barely populated.

Michener spent long hours talking with residents of the Keota area as he prepared *Centennial,* discussions he used as the backdrop for his retelling of the high hopes that came crashing down in the Dust Bowl days.

From Keota, the Pawnee Buttes are seen rising dramatically in the north. The Buttes, which Michener called "the twin sentinels of the plains," aren't easily accessible. Returning to Colo. 14, the route travels through the Pawnee National Grasslands, returned to their native state after the Dust Bowl era showed the danger of raising crops on portions of the High Plains. A small picnic ground just north of Briggsdale offers a good look at native prairie.

PLATTEVILLE

Fort Vasquez

On U.S. 85, one mile south of Platteville. Memorial-Labor Day: Monday-Saturday, 10–5; Sunday, 1–5.

☐ The site does not inspire thoughtful consideration of the story of Colorado fur trade, as cars and trucks speed by on both sides of the dusty, dry site.

The fort was built about 1835 by experienced mountain men to capture the Indian buffalo-robe trade along the South Platte. At least once the traders attempted to transport goods to St. Louis by river. Seven hundred buffalo robes and four hundred buffalo tongues were loaded on a flat-bottomed boat, but the crew had to wade and push for the first 300 miles.

The fort was reconstructed in the 1930s as a WPA project.

BURLINGTON

Kit Carson County Carousel

Burlington fairgrounds, 15th St. and Lincoln Ave. Burlington is near the Kansas border, off I-70. Open weekend evenings during summer.

☐ If you're coming in from Kansas along I-70, a stop at Burlington and a quarter will buy a nostalgic whirl on an historic carousel.

This is the land of homesteaders, where having a Saturday ice cream cone meant herding in the cows and milking them while someone else took the five-mile trip into town to buy ice from the man who had cut it in the winter and kept it under hay throughout the summer. Then home to layer it with the salt and churn it into dessert. The best part was that whatever was made had to be eaten on the spot.

This is land that appreciates the simpler pleasures, such as the joy of riding a carousel on a Saturday night.

The Kit Carson County Carousel is the only one of its kind and the oldest carousel still in operation. Its fantastic hand-carved menagerie includes lions, giraffes, tigers, camels, dogs, ponies, and hippocampi. Tunes from the 1909 Wurlitzer Monster Military Band Organ invite everyone to a faraway land where the sun always shines and the world is glorious. All for a quarter.

Country Inns of the Rocky Mountain West

by Doris Kennedy

Kennedy wants only the best for her readers. She not only visits every one of the inns in her comprehensive book, she also tries out their breakfast muffins, climbs red-carpeted turret staircases to investigate uppermost rooms, and sleeps in the Murphy beds. Along the way, she becomes friends with the innkeepers.

Her chatty descriptions share more information about an inn than most of us would gather if we were guests for a week. Along with a sketch of each inn and a complete rundown on its prices and facilities, we learn names of the children, favorite recipes, and the history of the hand-crocheted bedspreads atop guest beds. There's nothing more a traveler could ask for.

CHAPTER 7

SOUTHEAST

COLORADO SPRINGS

White House Ranch

*East entrance to the Garden of the Gods, off 30th St.,
Colorado Springs. Summer: Wednesday through
Sunday, 10–4; Labor Day to Christmas: weekends only.
578-6777.*

☐ There's not another museum like this one in
Colorado, or perhaps for many states. Set aside
a couple of hours, tie up your walking shoes,
forget the present, and be ready for a mind-
boggling walk through the trail of time.

The inhabitants who busy themselves on the
ranch grounds know nothing about the twentieth
century. They're always ready to quit their
chores and chat, but they're interested in what's
happening in Denver City, way up yonder, or in
the railroad that will soon span the continent.
Don't miss the opportunity to talk with these
hard-working pioneers.

Let's get the name straight first. White
House Ranch sounds suspiciously like a western
cousin of our president's White House. Forget
the connection. White House Ranch is a property
that is important to Colorado's heritage and is
named after one of its buildings, a large home
that just happened to be painted—you guessed
it—white.

The half-mile trail in this outdoor living history
museum carries its followers on an abbreviated
journey through Colorado's past. First the land
belonged to the Ute Indians, who might have wintered on the very spot. But their long-established
custom of using the Manitou Springs area as a
home base came to an end when homesteaders
of the 1860s pushed their way to the foothills.

Walking along the trail, you'll meet Indians, a homesteader, a rancher, and a wealthy suburban family – a microcosm of the development of Colorado Springs. The trail first passes right by Walter Galloway's cabin. He homesteaded the 160-acre tract of land that is now the White House Ranch. The government gave land to anyone who would live on it for five years and clear at least ten acres. Galloway is trying his best to get the land developed, so he often spends his days working with his scythe, saw, or hoe.

Life wasn't easy in a tiny, chinked cabin. Seven years after arriving, Galloway sold his 160 acres to the Chambers family for $1400. The trail now leads to the ranch they established.

Incredibly, the land that just barely supported Galloway was soon to produce enough to feed hotel guests in Colorado Springs. The Chambers lived on the ranch for twenty-five years; during that time Colorado became a state, gold was discovered in nearby Cripple Creek, and the luxuries of indoor plumbing and electricity became available.

Grasshoppers and lack of water were major problems, but the ambitious Chambers persisted. Wife Elsie wrote in a letter just eleven years after moving to the ranch, "The homestead claim has grown more fruit and vegetables than any other ranch in El Paso County. With its six acres of asparagus, hundreds of apple trees and hundreds of cherry trees, besides other fruit, its value has increased many-fold."

No one used factor-fifteen sunscreen in those days, so today fair-skinned, feminine field hands wear concealing bonnets and long skirts. Stable hands work with the animals, while in front of a blistering fire, a blacksmith fashions needed tools.

The Chambers sold their ranch in 1900 to General Palmer, the founder of Colorado Springs. He lived just to the north, in the beautiful Glen Eyrie mansion.

He built the three-story Orchard House on the newly acquired property. With a third floor set aside for servants, an informal morning room, and annunciator system, the house offered luxurious quarters on some of Colorado's most scenic real estate. This is the home that is today painted white, giving the area its name.

Slowly, the home is being restored and furnished. It's open for tours on certain days.

White House Ranch is not widely known outside Colorado Springs, perhaps because it is owned by the city and not as heavily promoted as a private site would be. Whatever the reason, it's the perfect complement to a tour of the Garden of the Gods, which is right next door.

Garden of the Gods_____

30th St. off Hwy. 24, Colorado Springs. Visitors' Center open summers, 8:30–5. 578-6939.

☐ No wonder Colorado gets rave reviews. Upturned red rocks thrust skyward at the very point where prairie grasses meet the evergreens of the Rampart Range mountains. Dramatic colors and fanciful silhouettes are at every turn.

Garden of the Gods has long been a meeting place, ever since the Utes wintered at nearby springs. They called it "the old red land" and often passed through it traveling on Ute Pass Trail.

Homesteaders, such as the one portrayed at White House Ranch next door, forced the Utes to Utah reservations in the 1880s, and the park passed into private hands before becoming a part of city park lands.

We can thank the mountain-building pressures that uplifted Pikes Peak for the Garden of the Gods' formations. The rocks that now stand nearly upright were horizontal sediments deposited by streams, winds, and seas over millions of years. The same pressure that formed the Rockies bent the sedimentary rock layers in the Garden, forcing them upward. Erosion, wind, and rain have sculpted them into their present shapes.

The Visitors' Center is the natural starting point for exploration. Slide programs on the park, brochures on horse trails, and well-done displays interpret the important geological and human history and share information on the area's plants (thousand-year-old trees) and wildlife (bighorn sheep in winter).

Daily summer programs include two interpretive walks along a paved trail, a patio program, and an evening program.

Miles of trails wind in and out of these red skyscrapers. Much of the most spectacular scenery is in the Central Garden Area, which can be seen along an easy, half-mile trail that leads to Three Graces and Cathedral Spires.

Balanced Rock and Steamboat Rock are two of the most popular formations. Balanced Rock is made of sandstone that was deposited by streams more than 250 million years ago. The rock layer underneath is softer and has been worn away until only a small support remains for the huge upper rock. It looks as if it could topple at any moment, but no one's taking any bets.

May Natural History Museum _____

710 Rock Creek Canyon. Four miles southwest of
Colorado Springs on Colo. 115 (Nevada Avenue). Daily
in summer. 576-0450.

☐ For some people, ladybugs are just about the
only insects worth bothering about. Miller moths,
grasshoppers, and all the rest are just a nuisance.
Not so for Mr. May, a former Canadian
forest ranger who began his collection in 1903.
The seven thousand tropical invertebrates on
display in this out-of-the-way museum are only
a fraction of his entire collection.

The family-run museum has locusts whose
wing colors shade from chartreuse to fuchsia;
moths resembling kitchen gadgets with sus-
picious-looking attachments; beetles with sixteen-
inch-long feelers, and fruit bats that, because
they need to take off from a gliding start (as
from a tree), frequently die in the attempt.

Most amazing are the seven-inch-long Indo-
nesian stick insects. Stick is too connotative of
substance: these are thinner than toothpicks, and
more like the width of a strong blade of grass.

The butterflies are startlingly beautiful and
adaptive. Owl butterflies look like owls; leaf
butterflies like leaves. The snakes, lizards, and
bats that enjoy butterfly appetizers are evidently
fooled by the big "eye" spots and miss the leaf-
like butterflies altogether. Perhaps the enormous
ten-inch wingspan of the Alexandria intimidates
its enemies.

The museum is also a study in changing
geopolitical boundaries, as many of the insects
were gathered from countries whose names are
now history. The cases display invertebrate
insects from around the world, from Guthrie,
Oklahoma, to Walayar Forests, India.

American Numismatic Museum_____

818 N. Cascade Ave., Colorado Springs. Tuesday-Saturday, 8:30–4. 632-2646.

□ Pleasures are often found in unexpected places. Here, in the nation's coin collectors' headquarters is a thorough and well-presented section on American coins, alongside a smaller exhibit on the history of coins worldwide. It's disconcerting to think about nickels without the White House, or quarters without eagles and without "In God We Trust" encircling the rim.

But imagine the early Continental dollars. The thirteen interlocking circles were connotatively appropriate, but to whom was the motto "Mind Your Own Business" directed? Even earlier shilling notes could be exchanged for Spanish milled dollars.

American politicians once used coins to get more mileage for their policies. In 1837, President Jackson and Congress disagreed over establishing a U.S. bank. Jackson took the initiative and struck a coin on which he is shown rising like a specter out of the roof of a four-story building brandishing a sword and saying, "I Take the Responsibility."

Cheyenne Mountain Zoo_____

Cheyenne Mountain Highway, west of the Broadmoor Hotel, Colorado Springs. Daily, 9–4:30. 475-9555.

□ The zoomobile is not just for the older set: anyone who has been to the mountainside zoo knows that it's a long climb up the trail. Summer visitors can save their energy by riding the zoomobile to the highest point and then enjoying a pleasant stroll, all downhill.

Maybe it's the 6800-foot altitude. Maybe it's the inspiring view. Whatever the reason, the animals are prolific. More than 140 giraffes have been born, and more orangutans have been produced at Cheyenne Mountain than in any other zoo in the world.

The zoo is unusual not only for straddling a mountain, but also because it does not receive any government funding. That makes its large collection of more than 800 animals in well-kept displays all the more impressive.

The zoo was started by Spencer Penrose, who was given gifts of animals by his worldwide circle of friends. His backyard didn't seem appropriate for the exotic breeds, so he kept them confined on the perimeter of the golf course until the zoo was built.

Many standard zoo varieties are here, including the Kodiak bear, black rhinoceros, black leopard, and Siberian tiger. But Cheyenne Mountain has many rare species as well. The Sumatran tiger, found in only two other zoos, recently produced a cub. The shy Bongo antelope is rarely found in captivity; so is the red panda.

A favorite collection is of the smartly dressed penguins, who wade in and out of their large indoor pool and spend their day eagerly awaiting the arrival of the lip-smacking fish, often fed to them by hand, to the delight of onlookers.

Colorado Springs Fine Arts Center_____

30 W. Dale St. Tuesday-Saturday, 9–5; Sunday, 1–5. 634-5581.

☐ This attractive museum by the riverside park is exemplary in its displays and its architecture. Everyone will enjoy the interior patio presided over by a tall Haida totem.

The totem's story is a good one. It once stood

proudly in the rain forests of the Pacific Northwest, but a combination of greed and cultural callousness somehow resulted in the carving being sent to a California lumber mill. How it was discovered and sent to Colorado is another story for the next edition.

The most famous collection is of santos and retablos, the primitive religious objects that were once common in the homes and churches of the Southwest.

Visiting the museum is fun, because there's just enough to see but not too much. Just down the hillside is a small outdoor botanical garden and acres of streamside grass.

El Pomar Carriage House Museum _____

Lake Ave. and Lake Circle, across from the Broadmoor Hotel, Colorado Springs. Tuesday-Sunday, 10–12 and 1–5. 634-5353.

☐ A five-star resort complex is an unlikely spot for this fine carriage collection, but the Broadmoor has never been one to stand by convention. The coaches belonged to the hotel's founder, as did the Indian costumes and artifacts that are also on display.

More than twenty spiffy carriages are immaculately preserved, painted, and polished. The Ladies Spider Phaeton is still elegant with its tufted beige velvet cushions. A gay-nineties surrey is trimmed in priceless bird's-eye maple.

It's as interesting to ponder the carriages as to wonder about the personalities and lifestyles of the many wealthy people who must have used them. The caretaker can be a source for some interesting stories, including the one about the black limousine that carried President W. H. Harrison to and from his fateful Inaugural Address.

Pioneers' Museum

215 S. Tejon St., Colorado Springs. Monday-Saturday, 10–5; Sunday, 1–5. 578-6650.

☐ Colorado Springs isn't just another pretty face with wide boulevards and graceful mansions. There's a history behind it all, well told by the Pioneers' Museum.

Beaded clothing and feathered headdresses recall that Indians were the first residents; it was their path that guided prospectors over what became Ute Pass. Furniture from author Helen Hunt Jackson's front room takes us back to Victorian days, as do the medical and dental supplies used when Manitou Springs was head-quarters for ailing easterners to take their cures. Pottery from the Van Briggle studio, still a going concern, is displayed as well.

McAllister House

423 N. Cascade Ave., Colorado Springs. Winter: Thursday-Saturday, 10–4. May through August: Wednesday-Saturday, 10–4; Sunday, 12–4. Groups welcome. 635-7925.

☐ General Palmer had great hopes for the city he founded, Colorado Springs. He sent for Henry McAllister, a young major who would help him build a vibrant city.

They started from scratch, living in flimsy wooden shanties and shivering through winter storms. One particularly bad windstorm blew a narrow-gauge train right off its tracks. That incident convinced McAllister that severe measures had to be taken to protect his family from the untamed Colorado elements.

He ordered workmen to build his new home with twenty-inch thick walls and to anchor the

roof into the brick with iron rods. His strategy
worked, and his home is one of the few surviving
from that era.

The elegant furnishings of the home made it
a showpiece of the city. Not only did it have
white marble mantelpieces brought from Phila-
delphia, it had running water. The home sat
almost alone in the prairie, waiting for the city
to grow up around it.

The Colonial Dames of America have supple-
mented original furniture to create an exceptional Victorian atmosphere in which the
McAllisters would have felt right at home. The
family Bible, with its handwritten notes on
home remedies on the inside cover, rests promi-
nently in the solemn parlor.

The quaint gardens carry through the Victorian
theme and provide welcome shade for weary
sightseers.

Prorodeo Hall of Champions & Museum of the American Cowboy _____

*I-25 at Rockrimmon Blvd., Colorado Springs. Exit 147
off I-25. Summer: daily, 9–5. Shortened winter hours.*

□ America's cowboys were as tough as the
steers they herded, as independent as the country
they roamed, as self-sufficient as the pioneers
that preceded them. Their role in the West has
become an American legend, feeding movies,
art, and novels.

The tasks that were once a part of the yearly
roundup have been refined. Steer roping has
become an art. So has bronc busting. Roundups
now take place on a small scale, amidst the
confines of barbed-wire ranches.

But rodeos, the showcases of cowboy skills,
attract hundreds of thousands of city folks.

Denver's National Western Stock Show and
Rodeo is held in January, and Colorado Springs's
Pikes Peak or Bust Rodeo in early August is
one of the oldest and largest in the state, with
top rodeo stock and big names.

Two multimedia shows begin the Prorodeo
Museum experience, bringing wild bulls far too
close for comfort. The films trace the history of
rodeo from early trail drives.

A finely designed museum offers a glimpse
into the stars of the rodeo world, their trophies,
and their prize possessions. Over eighty of the
rodeo greats, including Larry Mahan and Casey
Tibbs, receive special tribute.

Outside are the luxurious retirement quarters
of the animals who make the work of rodeo
heroes so tough: the bucking bull and bucking
bronc. A longhorn steer also lives here, representing the cattle that helped start the professional rodeo sport.

Ghost Town _____

Hwy. 24 W. and 21st St., Colorado Springs.
May 1–Memorial Day and Labor Day–mid-October,
Monday-Saturday, 9–1. Memorial Day–Labor Day,
Monday-Saturday, 9–6, Sunday, 1–6. 634-0696.

☐ Step back a hundred years when you pass
through the turnstyle, as this "town" shows life
just the way it was in Colorado during the
1880s and 1890s.

Every detail is authentic, down to the seashell that holds a door open in the crowded little
home out back. All the items were painstakingly
collected in Colorado by a local family during
the 1950s. Even the wood from the structures is
original, although some pieces were reduced in
size to fit into the old roundhouse, itself an
antique.

Along the perimeter are wooden storefronts. A peek inside reveals the intricacies of barber shops, jails, and drugstores with mysterious potions. Many stories could be told from the General Store alone, as it gives such a complete picture of everyday details. Resting on one corner of the dusty, wide-planked wooden floor is a Chinese laundry stove, with ten metal irons leaning on it to be warmed sufficiently to press petticoats and breeches.

Simple signs recall a day long gone. "Ice Cream on Saturday" conjures images of town kids, free from school on the weekend, turning the ice cream machine. Or perhaps it was on Saturday morning that the ice wagon made its rounds to the small town, or that a farmer brought cream to the store. Did people line up in anticipation? Was Cookies 'N Cream a favorite then as now?

Other signs promote less speculation but more nostalgia: "Eggs: 10¢ a Doz." "Milk: 20¢ a Gallon." An original Wells Fargo poster reads, "6 Days to Sacramento."

Various vehicles round out the collection. The stagecoach that ran between Denver and Cheyenne in 1868 was powered by four to six horses. Eleven passengers plus the driver and guard bounced along on leather springs. Deer-hide curtains provided a refined touch.

An adjacent building gives a more personal glimpse back in time. The kitchen of this repro-duced upper-middle-class home has a woodstove with yet more irons leaning on it, and a pie pantry covered with pierced tin. What a job it would have been to keep that full, especially without the help of Marie Callender.

Ghost Town is peppered with many entertaining ways to spend spare change. Peep

shows, shooting galleries, and electric pianos
keep children begging for more dimes.

Van Briggle Art Pottery

*600 S. 21st St., Colorado Springs. Open daily, except
Sunday. 633-7729.*

☐ Touring the Van Briggle studio is a Colorado
Springs tradition. The tour is brief, free, and
nonstrenuous. Perhaps therein lies its popularity.

The Van Briggle who started it all was an
accomplished potter who won many awards
before his death in 1904. His studio is still busily
turning out lamps, lampshades, ashtrays,
pitchers, and vases, all of which can be purchased at the gift store, where the ten-minute
tour ends.

U.S. Air Force Academy

*North of Colorado Springs, off I-25. Daily, 6 A.M.–5
P.M. 472-2555.*

☐ Nothing good happens quickly. It takes four
years to train an Air Force cadet, at least six
weeks to train the Academy's falcon mascots,
and a minimum of two-and-a-half hours to visit
the Academy. The tour is worth every minute.

The Academy's unrivaled setting at the base
of the Rampart Range and almost in the shadow
of Pikes Peak helps ensure that it remains Colorado's leading man-made attraction. Since the
Academy is a game refuge, hundreds of deer
and other animals enjoy the grounds in safety.

Tours start at the new visitor's center west
of the cadet chapel where they open with a
dramatic fourteen-minute film. Shown on the
half-hour, it sets the patriotic mood for the
day's visit.

The predominant theme of the display area
is "Commitment to Excellence" developed through

Academics, Military, Athletic, and Character
Development programs. Each of these themes
is illustrated through videos, photos, and text.
Both the exhibit area of the Visitor's Center
and the outdoor path leading to the chapel and
academic grounds are wheelchair accessible.
From the Center, guests may choose a self-tour,
using the maps available at the entrance gates
or Visitor's Center, or, during the summer, may
join a guided tour. These free, thirty-minute
tours start at 9:15 and run until 4 P.M., Monday
through Saturday. They give further information
on the Academy and walk through Arnold Hall,
the cadet social area, where a large cafeteria is
open to the public.

Some of the top attractions:

**The Thunderbird Airmanship Over-
look.** The Thunderbird Airmanship Overlook
offers a view of flying activities often glimpsed
from the interstate. There are also displays on airmanship programs and the USAF Thunderbirds.

Falcon Stadium. Falcon Stadium is the
scene of graduation day, when hundreds of caps
are tossed exuberantly in the air, and of the
football games where trained falcons perform
halftime feats. The Colorado prairie falcon is the
bird used by cadet falconers in flying demonstrations. For the last decade, most of the birds
used in public exhibitions have been produced
in the Academy breeding program.

The cadet area and chapel. The cadet
area and chapel is a main drawing card. During
the summer, free guided tours of the cadet area
leave from the Visitor's Information Booth every
half hour.

The chapel is a national landmark with its
seventeen gleaming aluminum spires reaching
150 feet upward. It is open to tour daily, except

when services are being held. Even then, the public is invited to join in the 9 A.M. and 11 A.M. Protestant and Catholic worship. The chapel is closed for a few special events and the week following graduation.

One of the most photogenic sights at the Academy is the Noon Meal formation, but this happens only on school days during the academic year. At 12:10 P.M. all 4417 cadets form into their forty squadrons and march across the ter- razzo to Mitchell Hall, the cadet dining area. The best viewing area is from the walkway north of the chapel.

Athletics. The Academy has 125 acres of athletic fields and an enormously impressive field house, with a 2500-seat ice rink and a 6000-seat basketball arena. The field house is also the place to find food for yourself but not for your car: there are no gas stations on the grounds.

North Pole/Santa's Workshop

Ten miles west of Colorado Springs on Hwy. 24. May- Christmas Eve. 694-9432.

☐ You can't miss the many billboards and brochures advertising this children's playland.

Whether or not you miss the "fairyland village" is probably dependent on the persistence of your children.

The younger ones will probably love the fun castle, miniature train ride, slide, and seventeen other rides. Parents appreciate the cleanliness. Even on the hottest of days, Santa sits by his cheery fireplace, his ample lap ready. His sleigh is always spic-and-span for photo sessions. Other prime targets for Instamatics are the well- dressed little gnomes and the pet reindeer.

Western Museum of Mining and Industry _____

Ten miles north of Colorado Springs at exit 156A off I-25. Daily, 9–4. 495-2182.

☐ The museum is dominated by the machinery of a ten-stamp mill from the 1890s, the only working stamp mill left from that frantic era. When the processor is switched on, the museum groans and shakes under its power.

Pikes Peak Auto Highway _____

Starts twelve miles west of Colorado Springs off U.S. 24. Open, weather permitting, May-November. 684-9383.

☐ The graveled toll road leading to the summit gives nerve-shattering views as it snakes its way up the northwest slope. A twisting carriage road was replaced by the present highway in 1915, thanks to the foresight of Spencer Penrose of Broadmoor Hotel fame. To gain publicity for the highway, Penrose inaugurated the Pikes Peak National Hill Climb Contest in 1916. This race continues to draw thousands every summer.

The famous road climbs 7309 feet in eighteen miles; although it's certainly safe, highway organizations recommend that only experienced mountain drivers attempt it. Including a very welcome stop to steady your nerves and refuel with strong coffee, the trip will take three hours.

Views of the Sangre de Cristo range and the Arkansas Valley are dramatic. The famous landmarks include the Cascade Burn, Glen Cove, and the Bottomless Pit.

MANITOU SPRINGS

Pikes Peak Cog Railway _____

515 Ruxton Ave., Manitou Springs. Round-trip, 3 hours, 10 minutes. May-October. 685-5401 for reservations.

☐ Ascending Pikes Peak isn't what it used to be. Zebulon Pike walked for days, only to find himself partway up with no socks, blankets, or food, and waist deep in snow. No wonder he turned back.

Today's intrepid tourist need brave no such hardships. A modern fleet of flaming-red railway cars allow travelers to lean back and enjoy the view.

Eight trains daily climb the world's highest cog railway route, departing from the quaint Manitou Springs station. On a busy day, the line transports 1500 passengers; during the summer rush, reservations are necessary.

The tracks parallel Ruxton Creek through Engelmann Canyon, named after one of the many pine varieties seen along the 7500-foot climb. At 11,578 feet, all trees are left behind. The final half-mile is through hostile tundra where sturdy, primitive plants hug the landscape, managing to grow about one inch every hundred years.

No matter that it's ninety degrees on the plains, chances are that the 14,110-foot summit wind chill factor won't be much above freezing. In fact, half an hour out of the station, passengers begin donning sweaters and parkas; when they disembark on the top, many wish for mittens as well.

The scheduled forty-minute layover is just long enough to enjoy the Summit House's melt-in-your-mouth donuts, a house specialty since 1915.

Mt. Manitou Incline_____

506 Ruxton Ave., Manitou Springs. Daily in summer.
685-9086.

□ The world's longest scenic cable railway
climbs to the 9000-foot summit of Mt. Manitou
every half hour. At one point the counterbalanced
cable cars tilt to a 68 percent grade.

At the end of the ride is a small restaurant
and unexcelled views for picnics and walks. The
evening "sequin" trip overlooks the city sparkling
3000 feet below.

Cave of the Winds_____

Manitou Springs. Forty-minute tours. 685-5444. Open
year-round, 10–5; summer, 9–9.

□ A crew of guides lead thousands of chilly
tourists through the labyrinthine groupings of
stalactites and stalagmites. Remember your
mnemonics here: it's the stalactites that hold on
tight to the ceiling and grow downward.

The cave has been popularized to the nth
degree. Every corner and cavern of the seven-
eighths-mile tour glows with pastel illumination
and each turn of the bend carries its own name:
Carrot Patch, Boston Alley, and so forth.

While it is nice to escape the summer heat for
a few minutes, some people really go over-
board on the underground atmosphere and get
married in the underground "Bridal Chamber,"
complete with its own red carpet.

Miramont Castle Museum _____

9 Capitol Hill Ave., Manitou Springs. Memorial Day-Labor Day: daily, 10–5; September-May: daily, 1–3. Self-guided audio tours. Groups welcome. 685-1011.

☐ A man's home is his castle, and when it has forty-six rooms, it deserves to be called one.

Miramont was built in 1895 during the Cripple Creek gold rush period by a French priest who lived in it with his mother. Later, the Sisters of Mercy ran it as a sanatorium and retreat for forty years.

Since the original furnishings are long gone, the castle's rooms now reflect the eclectic interests of a local historical group. Victorian Life Museum encompasses several furnished rooms. The Model Railroad Museum, open only in summer, is operated by the Golden Circle Mile Railroad Club, named for the two trains that went from Pikes Peak to Cripple Creek. Its trains tell the story of railroads in the region. A children's room, entered through a tunnel, displays antique toys.

The last stop at this four-story National Historic Site is usually the terraced Queen's Parlour Tea Room.

Manitou Cliff Dwellings Museum_____

Just north of Manitou Springs, off Highway 24. Mid-May–mid-October, 10–5, except Friday. 685-5242.

☐ McDonalds sells burgers on the Gaza Strip, London Bridge is in Arizona, so why not bring the Anasazi to the tourists in Colorado Springs?

That's just what enterprising citizens did in 1904 when they dismantled thousand-year-old structures from southwestern Colorado and glued them back together in Pikes Peak Country.

During the summer, Indian dances are desultorily performed; photos of the dancers cost extra.

MONUMENT

National Carvers Museum _____

14960 Woodcarver Rd., Monument. Exit 158 off I-25. Daily. 481-2656.

☐ Woodcarvers from across the nation send their best efforts to the museum for display. Some of them are expected (duck decoys), many of them are patriotic (busts of Lincoln, reliefs of the American flag), some are silly (wooden scissors) or even amusing (wooden neckties). The work of these patient artisans all oozes a homespun flavor, whether they're carving Indian chiefs or Bicentennial tributes.

In the hope that the collection proves an inspiration, carving tools are sold at the counter, and information on carving instruction is available.

FLORISSANT

Florissant Fossil Beds
National Monument _____

U.S. 24 out of Colorado Springs to the town of Florissant, then one mile south. Open daily, winter, 8–4:30; rest of the year, 8–7. 748-3253.

☐ Walking the park's paths is like going on a treasure hunt with no clues. In this case, visitors must accept the park rangers' contention that buried beneath the green valley grasses is the earth's most extensive fossil record of the Oligocene period.

Thirty-five million years ago, a twelve-mile-long lake filled the valley floor. Around it grew lush and lofty sequoias towering 300 feet. Over the next 500,000 years, millions of tons of dust and ash from nearby volcanic explosions filled the air, trapping or choking trees, leaves, insects, and fish. The ash has now become shale, and buried in its layers is a detailed record of ancient life.

Scientists have removed more than 80,000 specimens from this area in the shadow of Pikes Peak, including almost all the fossil butterflies of the New World.

The small and accessible visitors' center provides interpretation of the geologic history, as well as a good sampling of fossilized items: seeds, individual pine needles, fragile wings of insects etched on shale, and skeletons of now-extinct fish. Outside are more fossils: spectacular redwood stumps with astonishing thirteen-foot diameters.

During the summertime rangers give daily natural history programs and two-hour field exploration walks. Everything is covered by snow in winter, but the museum remains open. Cross-country skiers traverse 10.8 miles of well-marked intermediate trails.

Less than a mile north of the visitors' center, but still in the park, is the 1878 Hornbek Homestead. Its well, cellar, smokehouse, home, and barn are all reminders of pioneer life with its endless chores.

CRIPPLE CREEK

"Goin' up to Cripple Creek
    Goin' on the run...
Goin' up to Cripple Creek
    Gonna have some fun!"

Cripple Creek remains a fun place to go, even ninety years after those words were sung. It does not compete for the Coney Island of

Colorado title, as does another popular mining
town. True, Bennett Avenue is lined with little
shops selling hard ice cream, soft ice cream,
candy, yogurt, T-shirts, souvenirs, trinkets, and
antiques. But their presence hasn't obliterated
the character of this fine old town, known as
the world's greatest gold camp.

In 1890, cows had the run of this 9500-foot
basin. Then Cowboy Bob Womack discovered
gold, and within nine years, the area had nearly
500 mines producing about twenty million
dollars a year.

But Cripple Creek was more than just mines.
Its streets were literally paved with gold (low-
grade), and lined with department stores, a 150-
room hotel, dance schools, forty-nine grocery
stores, four book shops, and nine photographers'
studios.

The statistics are doubly impressive because
they can't be duplicated today by even the
largest of cities: five daily newspapers and fifty-
eight passenger-train departures daily.

Cripple Creek District Museums _____

At the head of Bennett Ave., Cripple Creek. Summer:
daily, 10–5:30. May and October: main building only.
November-April: main building open weekends. 689-2634.

☐ The frantic activity of this prosperous turn-
of-the-century town is well documented in the
three museums. The main twelve-room museum
highlights transportation, mining, and social
life. The threatening length of a teamster's whip
snakes around the baggage room; picks and
nine varieties of mallets remind us that miners
spent long hours chipping away at hard-as-rock
rocks. Third-floor displays of pioneer home
interiors are charming, with their brass foot-
warmers and seashell room dividers.

The second museum is in the Colorado
Trading & Transfer Building. The fifteen photo
panels are a good way to visually grasp the
history of the area: Men, all in hats, standing
four deep in a bar; the Fourth of July celebra-
tions with hundreds of flags; the pet burro
posing with the White House Saloon crowd.
The Assay Office, with its mining equipment,
is the final stop in this trio of museums.

The Imperial Hotel's
Victorian Melodrama

3rd St., Cripple Creek. Early June-Labor Day:
Tuesday-Saturday, 2 and 8:30; Sunday: 1 and 4:30.
471-8878.

☐ Cripple Creek has never ignored its cultural
life. Social activities once centered around the
opera house, which charged admission of up to
thirty-five cents. Any given week's bill might
include a musical concert, a couple of opera
performances, and a play.

Plays weren't taken lightly. The production
of *Uncle Tom's Cabin* in the spring of 1900 was
heralded by a noon parade with two bands, ten
Shetland ponies, bloodhounds, floats, and banners.

Just a twenty-five-minute train ride away was
Victor, with its own eight-hundred-seat opera
house. When lighter fare was called for, the
Crystal vaudeville was ready with three shows
nightly.

Good traditions die hard. The Imperial Players
have been presenting classic melodrama in
the Gold Bar Room Theatre since 1947. Each
season's play is from a nineteenth-century script,
widely different from the "mellerdrammer"
common throughout other western communities.

The plays have held up well during the
intervening hundred years. Good and evil are

refreshingly well defined, and although the characters are one-sided, the actors bring personality to the script.

The 285-seat theater is usually well filled but rarely sold out, so the play often can be seen on the spur of the moment. Plan on two-and-a-half hours of good entertainment with almost non-stop piano accompaniment.

Mollie Kathleen Gold Mine _____

On Hwy. 67, Cripple Creek. 689-2260.

☐ Authenticity abounds in Cripple Creek. The Mollie Kathleen was one of the major producers in its day, so the thousand-foot trip under Tenderfoot Mountain is the same one the miners took 361 days every year. Their days off were Labor Day, Christmas, New Year's, and Fourth of July.

Trips "in the cage" leave every five minutes for the descent and are guided by actual miners who explain the inner workings of a gold mine. Jackets make the mining experience more comfortable.

Cripple Creek and Victor Railroad _____

Daily in summer, 10–5. Departures every forty-five minutes. 689-2640.

☐ The train ride halfway to Victor and back (the train actually backs up on the return) costs 40 percent more than miners used to be paid for eight hours of labor in the underground mines.

But in those days, the train was a pass to the outside world, not just to the valley below.

Fifty-eight daily departures on three different lines connected Cripple Creek with its neighbors: All aboard at 1:30 P.M.

Anaconda	1:36
Beacon Hill	1:38
Elkton	1:42
Eclipse	1:45
Victor	1:51

Slender Pullman cars left Cripple Creek at 9 P.M., arriving in Denver early the next morning. The two-hour-plus, $2.50 round-trip between Colorado Springs and the gold camp was run four times daily by the standard-gauge Midland Terminal. Transportation was obviously a priority: in addition to all the trains, two electric trolley systems crisscrossed the district.

The narrow-gauge train whose whistle now echoes in the valley goes only a short distance, following scarred mining terrain where some of the richest ore ever mined was extracted and railed to Colorado City for milling.

The little train lumbers down the track, the diminutive 0-4-0-type engine pulling the tender, an observation car, and the popular open car. Views of the Arkansas Valley and multi-peaked Sangre de Cristo Range are in the background; the foreground is dotted with tailings, looking like mounds of golden-hued, gravel snow cones. Close enough to touch are thick aspen groves and white-blossomed thimbleberry shrubs.

Victor

Six miles south of Cripple Creek.

□ Victor is an almost-ghost-town that still has an authentic air about it. Its turn-of-the-century population of twelve thousand has dwindled to mere hundreds, but many proud buildings

persist, including the Victor Hotel, the Midland
Terminal Railway Station, and City Hall.
Overlooking the town with its empty lots and
steep dirt streets is Battle Mountain, dotted
with the silent towers of Ajax Mine, Portland
Mine, Independence Mine, and Strong Mine. One
block of Main Street is the Gold Coin Mine,
discovered while excavating for a hotel.

PUEBLO

Rosemount Victorian House Museum ___

*419 W. 14th St., Pueblo. June-August: Tuesday-Saturday,
10–4; Sunday, 2–4. September-May: afternoons only
except Monday. 545-5290.*

☐ Without a doubt, Thatcher's Rosemount is the
most lavish historical home to tour in Colorado.
But don't plan to peek inside at a frantic I-25
pace—the thorough tour of the thirty-seven
rooms lasts nearly ninety minutes.

The safe in John Thatcher's general store
was the only one in town, and everyone seemed
to have some spare money to safeguard in it.
Thatcher didn't have to think twice before
deciding to open a full-fledged bank, and the rest
is history.

Rosemount is an elegant showcase for the
Thatchers' exquisite taste. Margaret Thatcher had
a penchant for pink roses, and when Rosemount
was built in 1891, roses became a dominant
theme with pink roses on oval frescoed ceilings,
in the elegant fringed upholstery, decorating the
fine china, and growing in her greenhouse.

The stained glass flanking the grand oak
staircase is larger than that of many cathedrals,
but best of all is the luxury of the mansion's
detailing, from the carved wooden mantels of

the ten fireplaces to the mother-of-pearl inlaid headboard.

Three of the five Thatcher children never married. Lillian married in her late forties but divorced her husband after nine years and returned to Rosemount, where her bachelor brother Raymond also lived.

When he died in 1968, the three Thatcher children of Raymond's brother John relinquished their interest in Rosemount and its elaborate furnishings, and the gracious home opened to the public as a museum.

Home tours are always more interesting to adults – who like to admire fine furniture, Belgian lace, and elaborate decor – than to children. Whether or not this tour is for your entire family is up to you, but it's unparalleled for insight into a fine Front Range home of the 1890s.

Pueblo Zoo

City Park at Thatcher St. and Pueblo Blvd. April-September, 10–6; October-March, 9–4. 561-9664.

☐ In a country where bargains are rare, the Pueblo Zoo is a Great Find.

Happy Time Ranch is the children's portion but is a delight to all ages. The small-scale buildings appear so authentic that they could be part of an Elfin Farm. A picket fence surrounds a well-tended yard, chinked log cabin, well, out-house, and doghouse. A triangle hangs by the back door, waiting to call little elves to dinner.

Goats have the run of the ranch. They plead for treats, climb upon picnic tables, and sneakily lap up Shetland ponies' water.

A blue-muzzled llama shares a pen with two black-faced, docile sheep, while next door are caged bunnies and chickens. It couldn't be a better zoo farmyard.

The rest of the zoo animals are equally engaging: a gigantic Andean condor who needs to fly hundreds of miles instead of a few feet; a sun bear who gnaws at his tree, spitting out large chunks of wood; and Texas Longhorn cattle. The zoo is right inside the heavily forested City Park, on land that was once part of the Charles Goodnight Ranch. This is an appropriate location, as Goodnight blazed more than 2000 miles of cattle trails from Texas to Wyoming and is proudly remembered as the man who helped save the buffalo from extinction.

City Park Carousel _____

City Park, Pueblo. Across from zoo entrance. Open in summer.

☐ You know this carousel is special because it has its very own building. This "C. W. Parker #72 Carry Us All Three Abreast Carousel" was built in 1911 and has been enjoyed by Pueblo's children at the Minnequa Amusement Park since 1914. It has now been fully restored at an astronomical price, and its jumper horses are ready to please for another fifty years.

To ride a carousel is to see a dream spinning, although only carousel buffs know that merry-go-rounds move clockwise and carousels go counterclockwise.

At the turn of the century, as many as 3000 carousels may have been in operation across America. Now only about 250 remain.

As if thirty-six dancing horses weren't enough, a good collection of miniature amusement rides is right across the way.

El Pueblo Museum

905 S. Prairie, Pueblo. Summer hours: Tuesday-
Saturday, 11–3. 564-5274.

☐ El Pueblo is across the street from the Colorado State Fairgrounds, but for most tourists
the parking lot is more of a drawing card than
the museum.
The focal point is a full-size indoor reproduc-
tion of Fort Pueblo, where trappers and Indians
traded. But the museum exists largely to explain
the Fur Trade era to groups of schoolchildren,
who learn about the early mountain people and
Plains tribes.

CAÑON CITY

One mile off Highway 50, eight miles west of Cañon
City, two hours south of Denver. Bridge open year round.

Royal Gorge

☐ All the hype is directed to the bridge and
incline. After all, they're the ones that pay for the
billboards. Giving credit where credit is due,
this is the site of the world's highest suspension
bridge and the world's steepest incline.
But back to nature, and the gorge itself. This
remarkable canyon narrows at some points to
30 feet, while sheer cliffs rise 1200 feet above
the whitewater Arkansas, churning anxiously to
escape the rocky confines on its 1900-mile course
to the Mississippi.
Five-thousand-acre Royal Gorge Park may be
the only place in Colorado where a herd of deer
will stand still for petting. Park employees have
named each of these long-eared beauties.

Red Canyon Park

☐ Two other federal parks are nearby. Red Canyon Park has another of the state's natural red-rock outcroppings. A great place for photographers, there are also picnic grounds with grills and hiking trails. Reach it by traveling north on Fifteenth Street out of Cañon City and continuing twelve miles to the sign.

Temple Canyon

☐ Temple Canyon, six miles southwest of Cañon City, is reached from South First Street. Its hundred-foot amphitheater, set into a granite cliff, was thought by its discoverers in 1878 to be an Indian temple. The remote site can be reached in a little over an hour by following the trail at the Temple Ridge picnicground down to the bottom of the canyon and crossing Grape Creek.

SAGUACHE

Saguache County Museum

Highway 285, Saguache. Summers, 10–5.

☐ A stop in Saguache, with its wide main street and genuine log cabins sitting forgotten along back alleys, can be a welcome diversion in the San Luis Valley.

The museum building itself qualifies for history. It began as a schoolhouse more than 100 years ago, and then functioned as a jail, a courthouse, and even a home for the families of jailers.

Each room has a theme. The Pioneer Kitchen is hung with serious-looking implements that promise hard work in front of a wood-burning stove. The Spanish-Indian room holds rugs, santos, and pottery that reflect the heavy Spanish influence in the valley.

Since the building was Saguache's first school, the School Room is doubly authentic with its desks, organ, charts, slates, pictures, and teaching aids. Ask for a copy of "Rules for the Teacher."

The jail is almost too realistic with the likeness of Alferd Packer being guarded by Sheriff Wall, relaxing in an office chair. Packer's circumstances look ominous, what with all the handcuffs and leg irons; his real-life imprisonment in a now-extinct Saguache dungeon must have been just as bad.

ALAMOSA

Fort Garland_____

Twenty-five miles east of Alamosa. Memorial Day– Labor Day. Monday-Saturday, 10–5; Sunday, 1–5.

□ A cannon atop this impregnable adobe castle challenges miles of dry sagebrush and grasses. It's all peaceful now, but when the land belonged to the Utes, the fort's infantry and mounted riflemen were alert to danger.

Bent's Fort to the east had been a staging ground in 1846 for the taking of New Mexico. Although the United States then claimed southern Colorado, the Ute Indians had legal possession. When they successfully attacked Fort Pueblo in 1854, legendary Kit Carson was called in for a punitive expedition.

Fort Garland was established in 1858 as additional protection from Indian attack for the settlers of San Luis Valley. It wasn't until the remnants of the Ute tribes were removed after

Chief Ouray's death to dreary Utah and southern Colorado reservations that the fort was disbanded.

The historical museum has recreated the commandant's quarters as they appeared in 1866, the year that Carson commanded the fort.

Great Sand Dunes National Monument __

Thirty-two miles northeast of Alamosa.

☐ Pick any spring day in the San Luis Valley. Sun shining, no rain in sight, and a dry wind blowing across the uncompromisingly flat valley from the San Juans. Since little plant life exists to anchor the soil, the wind catches grains of sand that then sail a few inches before touching down and skipping a few inches farther, always heading northeast.

Bouncing along the earth in this haphazard fashion, the sand runs into the Sangre de Cristo, a solid wall of rock. The only indentation in this solid rock barrier is just north of Sierra Blanca, the range's highest mountain. In the turbulence created in rising over the pass, the wind loses much of its energy, dropping the sand at the foot of the pass.

Repeat this pattern for hundreds of centuries with billions of grains of dust and sand, and the result is the Great Sand Dunes.

The Dunes are not directly on the road to anywhere, but a detour is definitely in order. It's a place to hike, although not during the heat of a summer day, when the sun's trapped heat reflects in waves, even through thick-soled tennies. It's a place to learn and to experience the power of Colorado landscape from a new perspective.

The visitors' center is a must. Where else can you learn that only five plants grow in the dunes, or that two of its insects occur nowhere else in the world? All the animals that live in this arid home have drastically modified their behavior, especially the kangaroo rat, which has learned to survive without drinking any water.

The visitors' center is open all day, from 7 A.M. to 8 P.M. The next stop will be across Medano Creek and onto the dunes. A squishy round-trip to the summit of a nearby dune takes about three hours. That includes twenty stops for photos, eight "time-outs" to play beach by burrowing knee-deep in sand, and five swigs from the canteen across your shoulder.

Massive Sierra Blanca and the forbidding rocks of Crestone Needles overlook the sea of sand, making this desert among the most spectacular sights in Colorado.

ANTONITO

Cumbres & Toltec Scenic Railroad_____

Trains leave daily from both Chama, New Mexico, and Antonito, Colorado, mid-June through mid-October. Various packages available lasting from eight hours to overnight. P.O. Box 668, Antonito, CO 81120. (505) 756-2151.

☐ With all the commotion of taking on water and coal, it's good to hear the whistle blast four stern warnings. That's railroad code for "Get On Board."

Finally it's time to settle in the hard plastic seats to await arrival at the unlikely destination of Chama. Lurching along the narrow tracks at twelve miles an hour, there'll be time enough to see it all, whatever "all" encompasses.

Through an indecipherable loudspeaker, the conductor mumbles something about sitting back and relaxing to enjoy the scenery. We look, and indeed, the profusion of Indian paint-

brush, snowsquaw, and strawberry cactus is
staggering.

During the lazy sixty-four-mile trip, which
weaves eleven times across the deserted Colorado–New Mexico border, the train meanders
from silvery aspen groves to lush green fields
often spotted with hundreds of white sheep.
Later the train climbs along the rim of Phantom
Canyon, where twenty-million-year-old rock
sentinels rise above foaming waters.

The locomotive lumbers to a halt at Sublette
to take on water. Before it stops, it gives a
warning toot, and a herd of cattle kicks up its
heels in surprise and trots to a farther meadow.
The sooty camp of Sublette that once was a
temporary home to a hundred maintenance men
is now no more than five tottering buildings and
a water tank.

The train coming from Chama meets the
Antonito train at Osier, the only place in America
where two steam engines meet and exchange
locomotives. Soot-covered and a little restless,
everyone clambers out to stretch and breathe in
the bracing air.

The thirsty train that devours coal takes on water once more at the summit of Cumbres and then descends the 4 percent grade into Chama, but an hour away. A heavy drowsiness has settled on the passengers. Those who were exclaiming at every turn in the morning are now dozing or desultorily fingering their souvenir booklets.

When the whistle steams for the last time, it's a shock to see the jumbled rail yard, jammed parking lots, neon signs, and paved streets. All that had been left behind for a glorious day of chugging through the wilderness at a nineteenth-century pace.

TRINIDAD

Baca House and Bloom House _____

300 E. Main St., Trinidad. Daily guided tours from Memorial Day-Labor Day, Monday-Saturday, 10–4; Sundays 1–4. (719) 846-7217.

☐ The Santa Fe Trail was cluttered with oxen, cattle, mules, and weary travelers on horse, wagon, and foot. So it's a little surprising that two of Trinidad's grand homes were built just a front yard away from the dusty turmoil. Both are seen on the same tour, beginning with the Baca House.

Thick adobe walls, almost-spartan furnishings, kerosene chandeliers, wall-hung retablos, and wide-plank floors distinguish this 1869 home.

The Bacas were a prosperous Hispanic family of eleven. Señor Baca was an industrious New Mexican trader who traveled from New Mexico to Denver as early as 1860, bringing supplies to the just-founded mining camp on the banks of Cherry Creek. After seeing the Purgatoire River Valley, he convinced several New Mexican families to homestead the area with him the following year.

The Bloom House has scarcely any similarities to its neighbor, although it was built only thirteen years later, in 1882. By then the railroad had arrived, and all the bric-a-brac of the Victorian era was available to eager, upscale households.

Perhaps the most telling feature of this genteel period is at the front door. Upon entering a small vestibule, two doors blocked further entrance. Guests were ushered through the right-hand door into the formal parlor, sealed off from the rest of the house by a wooden sliding door. Family entered the left-hand door, which opened to the rest of the home.

The cutting garden in the Bloom's backyard is made for strolls and picture taking.

Former servants' quarters and stables house the Pioneer Museum, which is a collection of buggies, tools, and other early necessities.

LA JUNTA

Koshare Indian Museum _____

115 W. 18th St., La Junta. June-August, daily, 12–5; Saturday 10–5; September-May, 12–5. 384-4801. Koshare Indian dance performances given mid-June through mid-August on Saturday nights and selected weekdays. Call for schedule.

☐ Politicians and service groups like to recognize outstanding youths. So it's no surprise that the Explorer Post 2230 has its share of plaques on the wall. But no amount of recognition, even though some of it comes from President Reagan and Senator Bill Armstrong, prepares visitors for the home of the most famous Boy Scout troop in the world.

Buck Burshears founded the group in 1933. His lifelong interest in Indians found a natural outlet with his troop of enthusiastic teens. His skill in researching Indian customs, his love of children, and his natural leadership qualities all contributed to the development of the troop's achievements. Before long, the troop of some fifty boys had a repertoire of one hundred authentic Indian dances and was performing throughout the world.

Buck still takes an active role with his present troop of about forty-five boys, each of whom makes his own costumes for the dances. The troop's traveling has been drastically curtailed by rising transportation costs, but it is still invited to perform for conventions and special events. Most of its fifty yearly performances, however, take place in the fabulous kiva they have built adjoining their museum.

A kiva, an Indian ceremonial building, is circular. As is this one. But this is the largest kiva in the world. The tremendous roof architecture is unique to the Koshare Kiva. Forty tons of logs crisscross one another in the elaborately beamed ceiling. Subtle Indian paintings cover the ten wall panels. Built-in benches line the circumference; they are often filled to their 500-seat capacity for summer performances. The kiva is also often lined with the sleeping bags of schoolchildren from across Colorado who come to view the performances, as well as with traveling Scout troops.

Astonishment and pride over the achievements of Explorer Post 2230 increases when touring their museum, a museum whose initial construction was paid for by money earned from dance performances. Over the years, collectors have added their own treasures to the Koshare collection of artifacts and paintings.

The museum is one of the finest Indian museums in the United States, with several million dollars of items representing many North American tribes. Many examples of quillwork embroidery show the Indians' skill at decorative work before beads were available. The basket collection is one of the world's largest.

Buck Burshears and the boys who have worked so hard to perfect their Indian dances have put La Junta on the map; dance days have made the city a favorite detour for hundreds of thousands of tourists.

Bent's Old Fort National Historic Site___

Eight miles east of La Junta on Colo. 194. June-August, 8–6; September-May, 8–4:30. 384-2596.

☐ Driving east of La Junta toward the fort, past farmhouses hidden among clumps of cottonwood and railroad cars converted to barns and storage sheds, the old Santa Fe Trail seems to come alive. The flat prairie, with its heat, its meadowlarks, and its vast plains, brings thoughts of pioneers to mind.

The fort appears off to the right, its weather-faded flag hanging limply in the hot, still air. The short walk from the parking lot, with ninety degrees of May heat bearing down, reminds visitors of the many hardships met by the early

traders who traveled hundreds of miles to the
fort with their pelts.

Bent's Old Fort, built in 1833, became the
most important trade depot between Independence, Missouri and Santa Fe. For some
seventeen years, the Bent brothers and Ceran
St. Vrain maintained a giant commercial empire,
as Indian and American goods from the entire
Midwest passed through the fort's stockade.

The fort began as a trading fort, but its last
years were under military hands when the United
States fought Mexico in 1846. The Bents and
St. Vrain eventually found themselves between
a rock and a hard spot. Indians were resentful
of the influx of settlers, adventurers, and gold
seekers, and invading whites drove off bison,
recklessly used precious firewood, and fouled
the few watering places.

Although the demise of the fort is a sad
story, the reconstructed fort is a glorious site.
Costumed interpreters hammer in the carpenter
shop, make new fittings in the blacksmith shop,
stoke the courtyard fire with its hanging, black-
ened coffee pot, and tend the livestock.

All the rooms are open, and visitors inspect
the Mexican quarters with corner adobe fireplaces, the military quarters furnished with
massive trunks, and the trappers' quarters,
hung with boldly striped Hudson Bay blankets.

Two bastions and a watchtower give the fort
a medieval look; today both offer fine views of
the tamed prairie. From the second floor one
looks across the landscape and then down to
the plaza with its large fur press.

This bleak, dreary outpost, vulnerable to fierce
winters and sweltering summers, offered a
rough yet vital shelter during the taming of the
West. To the travelers of the twentieth century,
it is a welcome addition to the nation's heritage.

People of the Moonshell:
A Western River Journal

by Nancy M. Peterson

The land surrounding the Platte is dull, dry, and monotonous, but the Platte, which Indians called "Moonshell," was the lifeblood of the pioneers: the most significant route west was along its banks.

In well-written style, Nancy has captured the river's history in dramatic narratives about the individuals who boated, tracked, traversed, and cursed the Platte on their way west.

INDEX

ABOUT THE AUTHOR

Susan Kaye, a Denver native, is a travel writer whose articles have appeared in major periodicals and newspapers throughout the United States, Canada, and Europe. Her first book, *Small People in Colorado Places*, is currently in its fourth printing.

Kaye has also taught business technical writing at the University of Denver and the University of Colorado. She holds an MA in secondary education and is a frequent lecturer for youth and parenting groups.

Share the adventures—order additional copies of *The Best of Colorado* for family and friends.

Also by Susan Kaye, with children in mind: *Small People in Colorado Places*—newly revised and updated, now available from Pruett Publishing.

A whimsical, refreshingly honest guide for everyone who wants to explore Colorado with children, *Small People in Colorado Places* is a potpourri of adventures for families. Even long-time residents will be amazed at the hundreds of unusual activities available to families in Colorado.

Pruett Publishing Co. • 2928 Pearl St. Boulder, CO 80301 • (303) 449-4919

Please send me:

_____ *The Best of Colorado* @$8.95 ea.*

_____ *Small People in Colorado Places* @$8.95 ea.*

Name _____

Address _____

City_____ State _____ Zip _____

Payment enclosed $_____

Mastercard ☐ or VISA ☐ Exp. Date_____

Card Number _____

Signature _____

*Colorado residents please add appropriate sales tax. Pruett pays shipping charges on all orders accompanied by payment or charge card information. Prices subject to change.

☐ Please send me your complete catalog and add my name to your mailing list.